T0146807

Praise for *Take Charge of Your Life*

"Choice theory can unleash creativity to help you break old patterns, reframe problems into opportunities, and realize there is more than one right answer."

—Cheryl Grills, PhD, CTRTC

"This book is a 'game changer' for anyone ready to become the Captain of their own ship. Going far beyond theory and philosophy this powerful book is a hands-on guide to creating, rather than just observing one's life. A must read and more than once".

—Dr Phil McGraw, Host of the nationally syndicated series *Dr. Phil.*

Professional Recognition of William Glasser, M.D

Since 1989, Dr. William Glasser has been recognized as a member of the distinguished faculty of pioneers in the psychological professions by the renowned Evolution of Psychotherapy Conference of the Milton Erickson Foundation.

In 1990, he was awarded the honorary degree Doctor of Humane Letters, Honoris Causa, from the University of San Francisco.

In 2002, he received the California Association of School Counselors award for his many years of contributions to the school counseling profession.

In 2003, he was presented with the American Counseling Association Professional Development Award in recognition of his significant contributions to the field of counseling.

The American Counseling Association presented him with a Legend in Counseling Award in 2004 for developing reality therapy.

In 2005, the American Psychotherapy Association presented him with the prestigious Master Therapist designation.

Also in 2005, he was presented with the Life Achievement Award by the International Center for the Study of Psychiatry and Psychology for his enormous influence as a psychotherapist and author.

In 2006, he was awarded the honorary degree of Doctorate of Education from Pacific Union College in Angwin, CA.

In 2008, the European Association for Psychotherapy publicly recognized reality therapy, which Dr. Glasser developed, as a scientifically validated psychotherapy and was officially announced at the twenty-ninth Annual William Glasser Institute International Conference held in Edinburgh, Scotland, in 2009.

In 2010, Case Western Reserve University conferred the Distinguished Alumni Award upon him.

TAKE CHARGE OF YOUR LIFE

Also by William Glasser, MD

Choice Theory: A New Psychology of Personal Freedom

Reality Therapy: A New Approach to Psychiatry

Every Student Can Succeed

For Parents and Teenagers: Dissolving the Barriers between Them

Eight Lessons for a Happier Marriage

Warning: Psychiatry Can Be Hazardous to Your Mental Health

What Is This Thing Called Love?

Getting Together and Staying Together

Staying Together

Counseling with Choice Theory, the New Reality Therapy

The Language of Choice Theory

Positive Addiction

Fibromyalgia: Hope from a Completely New Perspective

Schools without Failure

The Quality School

The Quality School Teacher

Choice Theory in the Classroom

The Identity Society

The Choice Theory Manager

Available through wglasserbooks.com

TAKE CHARGE
OF YOUR LIFE

How to Get What You Need
with Choice Theory Psychology

William Glasser, MD

Revised and updated by Carleen Glasser, MA, CT/RTC

iUniverse, Inc.
Bloomington

Take Charge of Your Life
How to Get What You Need with Choice Theory® Psychology

iUniverse Star
an iUniverse, Inc. imprint

iUniverse books may be ordered through booksellers or by contacting:

iUniverse
1663 Liberty Drive
Bloomington, IN 47403
www.iuniverse.com
1-800-Authors (1-800-288-4677)

ISBN: 978-1-938908-32-3 (sc)
ISBN: 978-1-938908-33-0 (e)

Library of Congress Control Number: 2013903897

Printed in the United States of America

iUniverse rev. date: 7/8/2013

To our grandchildren, in whom our future lies:
Jana, Nate, Julianne, Jared, Rachel, Conor, Michael,
Lucy, Amelia, Nicholas and Scarlett.

Contents

Foreword

Jenny, serving a life sentence in prison, lashes out at other inmates and corrections officers on a daily basis as she tries to find meaning and purpose in what is left of her life. What does she have in common with Michael, in his last year of college, who is barely able to make it to class as he struggles with his mother's latest hospitalization for attempted suicide? Or with Jessica, a senior in high school, who is college bound but often self medicates with marijuana to ease immobilizing anxiety associated with her contentious relationship with her mother. Or Sylvia, divorced for five years, who finds herself in yet another unsatisfying relationship but hangs on even though sadness and despair are her only companions. Or Ms. Edna, retired and on a fixed income, who fights sleepless nights and constant headaches after recently joining the legions of inner-city grandmothers raising their incarcerated children's children. Or Charles, who entered his new position as department head with more than a little trepidation and has constant body aches and pains from the stress of managing a team that is anything but cohesive and effective. Or a group of social service supervisors who sit guarded, angry, and frustrated at a county training session as they bemoan the difficulty of managing overworked and under-resourced social workers in their agencies. What do all of these people have in common? An amazingly similar transformative response to choice theory.

In each of these situations, I personally witnessed the diminishing returns of external control and the liberating power of choice theory. Knowledge is power, and knowledge creates choice. Armed with insights into the what and how of human behavior, Dr. Glasser's simple yet elegant truths revealed a new way for them to understand themselves, others, and their choices in life. In each scenario, peoples' need for love, belonging, power, fun, security, and freedom struggled for fulfillment in a world filled with external control. Not only did they feel stifled by others, they were also the protagonists of external control. Their frustration skyrocketed when others didn't respond to "their" external control beliefs and maneuvers. Choice theory helped them make sense out of nonsense, established order where things seemed out of control, and reinstilled a sense of fulfillment where despair had become the norm. I introduced them to choice theory, whose basic principles had immediate, intuitive appeal and brought noticeable results.

In *Take Charge of Your Life: How to Get What you Need with Choice Theory Psychology*, Dr. Glasser presents a clear, no-frills explanation of choice theory and provides a wealth of examples to bring the theory to life. The vignettes and stories reveal the truths of his philosophy. Through choice theory, personal freedom and choice are regained. Where self-awareness was absent or mystifying and interpersonal relationships were all but in shreds, tattered by external control behavior, new insights and new ways of engaging emerge. Where hope faded, personal control was lost, misery prevailed, and the best behavior in our repertoire created more harm than good, new insights from a psychology of personal freedom increased understanding of self and others. Ultimately, Dr. Glasser shows how people can move closer to the one thing most important to our well being—better quality relationships with the important people in our lives.

Choice theory offers a science of human behavior and principles for regaining and maintaining internal control. It presents new opportunities for prevention *and* intervention with individuals, families, and groups. It offers tools for fostering quality communities. Most importantly, it is a powerful tool for cultivating resilience and renewing optimism for a life-affirming world that can promote well-being. It provides direction for the critical work of building a sense of community in schools and neighborhoods. As Dr. Glasser once said, "The community approach is the only way we can move the flat line of human progress upward."

In my three decades in clinical practice and community psychology, I have never been more impressed or affected by a theory and approach as I have by Dr. Glasser's simple yet elegant science, which explains how people can get along better with each other. External control psychology has become so ingrained in the fiber and fabric of human life that our senses and consciousness have been dulled to its pervasive presence.

Whether I am applying the principles of choice theory with my son, teaching it in an undergraduate course, or training managers and staff in community-based organizations, the effects are the same. It makes sense. It yields insights. It inspires positive behavior change and mental health. From teaching choice theory to women in prison to exposing parents and high school students to choice theory in a college-bound program, I continue to marvel at how it resonates with such a diverse cross-section of people, situations, issues, cultural affinities, and circumstances. Dr. Glasser is correct. Teaching people the limitations of external control and the advantages of internal control through choice theory leads them to the heart and soul of successful, happy lives.

In these times of great social injustice, poverty, and strife, times that can try one's soul, choice theory can be liberating. Dr. Glasser counsels that, regardless of circumstances, it does people no good to accept misery or blame it on the world. "To do so deprives them of all the opportunities they desperately need to take charge of their lives."

In choice theory, he offers a model of real empowerment. In his own words, "When you put choice theory to work in your life, you will spend your energy attacking the problem, not blaming it." In *Take Charge of Your Life*, Dr. Glasser shows how choice theory can unleash creativity—break patterns, reframe problems into opportunities, and realize that there is more than one right answer.

The African proverb states, "A person is a person because there are people." In other words, ultimately, at our core, we are social beings and quality relationships are paramount to our health and wellness. Thank you, Dr. Glasser, for having the creative genius to reorganize external control psychology into a psychology of internal control capable of nurturing quality relationships and communities. Through the liberating force of choice theory, we can freely become engaged in life-affirming, need-fulfilling relationships with family, friends, coworkers, communities, and the global village.

Cheryl Tawede Grills, PhD, CTRTC
Associate Dean, Bellarmine College of Liberal Arts,
Loyola Marymount University
President, The Association of Black Psychologists
Founder and Executive Director, Imoyase Community Support Services

Preface

When I began my psychiatric practice in 1955, I had already developed a more practical approach to psychotherapy. My psychiatric supervisor at the time, G. L. Harrington, and I had developed concepts that deviated widely from the generally accepted thinking. We based our ideas on our daily practice and tested their validity in our personal experience, as the modern tools of psychological research were not available. Since training in clinical medicine and psychiatry were based on an oral tradition as well as on known facts, we did not think there was anything unusual about our method. I began to write down my accumulated ideas, and people began to ask me to speak at meetings and to teach seminars. Eventually, we formed the William Glasser Institute to teach my ideas to people who wanted to use them.

My friends tended to prefer practical books that seemed accessible to the general reader. After many requests over the years, I have decided that now is the time to revise and reissue *Take Effective Control of Your Life*, originally published by Harper Collins in hardcover, and *Control Theory*, the same book published with a different title in soft cover.

My revisions reflect my current thinking based on my 1998 book, *Choice Theory: A New Psychology of Personal Freedom*. The current book does not replace *Choice Theory*. It essentially explains why and how, as a new psychology, choice theory can help people take charge of their lives by completely rejecting the world's most destructive and divisive psychology, external control.

The title *Control Theory* was misleading and confusing, so I changed the name of the approach to *choice theory psychology* in 1996. Now choice theory is taught all over the world as a new psychology based on the fact that we choose all we do, and the only person's behavior we can control is our own. That's why this book is titled *Take Charge of your Life: How to Get What You Need with Choice Theory Psychology*.

My wife, Carleen, has carefully reorganized and edited the book to maintain its integrity by present editorial standards. I have read what she has put together with my revisions to reflect the concepts of choice theory psychology, and I agree with what she has done here. This is a good book. I hope you enjoy reading it again if you read the original version. If you are a newcomer to these ideas, I would like to invite you to join us in making the effort to change how the world operates. I suggest we reject external control psychology and embrace our individual internal drive to connect with one another by practicing choice theory psychology.

By choosing to take charge of your own life with choice theory psychology, you can become a part of the equation that adds happiness and connection to the world in which we live now and to the world of future generations.

Acknowledgments

I would like to express my most sincere appreciation for William Glasser Institute Executive Director, Linda Harshman, who encouraged me to rewrite this popular book from our past. She has been telling me for years that this book is her own personal favorite. I have almost always listened to her suggestions, and now is no exception. I value her ideas and her loyal service to the William Glasser Institute for the past twenty-five years.

I sincerely appreciate Jim Coddington for all his help at William Glasser, Inc. and his earnest devotion to promoting my work.

I also would like to thank Reinfredo Perandos, who has contributed much to my care and made this rewrite flow effortlessly with his skillful contributions.

Shearon Bogdanovic gladly agreed to assist with the organizing and editing required to republish this book. Her work on the manuscript was invaluable to the completion of this project. She is also a respected faculty member of the William Glasser Institute and one of my most enthusiastic students.

Finally, I am indebted to my wife, Carleen Glasser, for all the work she put into this book and the love she brings into my life. She is a take-charge kind of woman, and I place myself in her loving hands daily. Thank you, Carleen, with all my heart.

Introduction

Psychology is the science that explains how people get along with each other. The present psychology of the world, external control psychology, is based on the assumption that, like machines, we can control one another. We attempt to control through any number of so-called motivational strategies or events, such as rewards and punishments. External control is very harmful to the relationships we all need, often to the point of destroying them. In contrast, choice theory psychology is based on the assumption that each individual, ultimately, controls only him or herself and is self-motivated.

The intrinsic nature of our motivation is derived from my understanding of the structure and function of the brain and based on our biological origins. Our genes, the biological building blocks of our bodies and minds, are nothing more than a series of molecular codes. They include the information for the structure and function of our brains, and we must follow their instructions if we are to survive and prosper. We become aware of many of our brain's genetic instructions as spontaneous pictures that appear in our minds—pictures that must be satisfied through the way we live our lives. Driven by our genes, we are captive to these pictures, but what we need to learn is that we are not captive to how we attempt to satisfy

1

them. We almost always have choices, and the better the choice, the more we will be in charge of our lives.

As explained in my 1998 book *Choice Theory: A New Psychology of Personal Freedom*,[1] choice theory is diametrically opposed to external control, because choice theory brings people who use it closer together; external control drives them further apart. I advocate that we give up external control completely and replace it with choice theory so that we can do something we have failed to do so far: improve the way we get along with each other. Using choice theory on a wide scale would result in better marriages, happier families, more successful schools, and increased quality in the workplace. Christakis and Fowler, in their contemporary review of the research in human relationships, said, "Psychological research suggests that feelings of loneliness occur when there is a discrepancy between our desire for connection to others and the actual connections we have."[2]

Most of us have had the experience of trying to console a friend who is trying to deal with a sudden and unexpected marital breakup. She repeats over and over again, "How could he do this to me? How can I start all over again at my age? What right has he to destroy everything we worked for all these years?" As time passes, it is clear to everyone but the friend that she is choosing to remain hostage to a marriage that is over.

All of us have lived through times like this—suddenly the picture we have of our life is very different from the picture we want, and we feel as if we have lost control of our lives. We believe things are hopeless, and we don't know which way to turn. What never occurs to us in these desperate situations is that we are choosing the misery we are feeling, and better choices are available if we can learn how to make them.

In this book I explain that we are not controlled by external events, difficult as they may be. We are motivated completely by forces inside ourselves, and all of our behavior is our attempt to control our own lives. When, for example, we blame our misery on a child, spouse, or parent, we are acting as if they, not we, are in control of our lives. Our friend did not have to be miserable when her husband left—she chose to be miserable in a desperate but ineffective effort to regain control over a part of her life she believed was slipping away.

This book will teach you how you can take charge of your life using choice theory psychology. You will learn to make more effective choices than the painful, ineffective ones that too many of us now make as we attempt to satisfy powerful and unrelenting needs within us. But to learn choice theory, you will have to give up your lifelong commonsense belief that almost all you do is a reaction or response to events around you.

For this reason, you may notice that I use some words differently than you may be used to. For instance, *depression* becomes *depressing*, *guilt* becomes *guilting*, and so forth. By transforming these static words into actions that more accurately reflect choices, I hope to imply that these behaviors are subject to change. As you transform your life using a choice theory point of view, you will see that this use of language helps to keep your thoughts more flexible.

This transition will not be easy. Lifelong beliefs, especially if they are held by almost everyone you know, die hard. I encourage you to be skeptical. Believe nothing in this book, no matter how persuasive my argument, unless you try it out in your life and discover it works for you.

1. Everything We Think, Do, and Feel Is Generated by What Happens Inside Us

We are in your car and come to a red light. You stop, and I ask you why you did this. You point to the red light and say, "It turned red—I always stop at red lights." Later your telephone rings, you answer it, and I ask why you picked it up. "Because it rang," you say and start to wonder what kind of fool I am. But am I really as foolish as you think? Do you always stop for red lights and answer the telephone when it rings? Haven't you ever run a red light purposely for what you considered a good reason—perhaps an emergency? Don't you sometimes pay little attention to a ringing phone because you are doing something better at the time?

I don't claim that the red light or the ringing phone have nothing to do with stopping and answering, but they are not what *cause* us to stop or answer. We stop because we all carry around inside of us a powerful desire to do all we can to stay alive. We pick up the phone when it rings because most of us have a strong desire to talk to anyone who wants to talk to us. Just think about the possibility of crashing at a busy red light or letting the phone ring when you are home alone with nothing to do, and it will become apparent that what moves you to act is inside, not outside, of yourself.

Nothing we do is caused by what happens outside of us. If we believe that what we do is caused by forces outside of us, we are acting like dead machines, not living people. Because we are alive, we can choose whether or not to answer the phone depending on whether or not it fulfills a current goal. In fact, what I will explain in this book is that everything we do—good or bad, effective or ineffective, painful or pleasurable, crazy or sane, sick or well, drunk or sober—is done to satisfy powerful forces within ourselves.

A telephone-answering device is a dead machine. It has no choice but to answer the phone. Its actions are controlled by the outside ring, and its sole purpose, put into it by design, is to respond without question to that ring. It is truly a slave as only a robot can be. But if we believe that, like machines, we are controlled by outside forces, whether those forces are as simple as a red light or as complex as a tyrannical boss, and give up the idea that we always have choices (limited as they may be), we embrace slavery.

If I believe that the motivation for all I do, good or bad, comes from within me, not from the outside world, then when I am miserable, I cannot claim that my misery is caused by uncaring parents, a boorish spouse, an ungrateful child, or a miserable job. If I were a machine, this claim might be valid. I could be programmed to feel good only if those I needed treated me well. But I am not a machine, and although I strongly desire good treatment from everyone in my life, if I don't get what I want, *it is my choice* whether or not to be miserable. The fact that it does not seem as if I choose my misery does not make it any less a choice. Again, to refute our old friend common sense, you can no more *make* me miserable than you can *make* me answer the telephone.

By now you may be taking strong exception to my claim that we choose most of the misery we feel. I know that when you lose a good job, it feels as though you've been pushed off a cliff. Everything you have learned all your life tells you that you are not choosing your misery—it is caused by your being out of work. I am sure you are also thinking, *It's bad enough that I've lost my job; how could choosing misery make it better?* I promise if you will give me time to prepare the groundwork, I will explain in detail why I make this claim and how you can use this knowledge to take charge of your life more effectively.

But for now, can you think of at least a few people you know who have made better choices than misery when they have been laid off from a good job? Somehow, without fear or resentment, they dealt with this situation as a challenge and chose not to be overwhelmed. To become more effective, you must learn what these people have learned: how you feel is not controlled by others or events. You are not the physical or psychological slave of your parents, husband, wife, child, boss, the economy, or anything else unless you *choose to be.* Later, I explain much more about why a person might choose to be miserable if other people don't treat him the way he wants to be treated. It turns out that choosing misery may be, at least for a while, a good choice. What is important to learn now is that it is always a choice and, over time, almost always a poor choice.

My cousin tells a joke about a young man visiting a large civic cactus garden in Arizona during the summer. Everyone admiring the cacti, including the young man, is lightly dressed because of the heat. Suddenly he jumps into a large patch of low cacti and rolls around on the spines. Horrified, the others quickly pull him out, but not before he has become a bloody mess. When they ask why he jumped in, he says, "It seemed like a good idea at the time."

Haven't we all done our share of cactus rolling? Stop and think of the last foolish thing you chose to do; didn't you do so because at the time it seemed like a good idea? While what we do always seems sensible to us when we do it, even a moment later it may seem like the stupidest thing we could have done. Therefore, good or bad, everything we do is our best choice at the moment. Even though I often say, "I knew it was foolish when I did it," the facts are, foolish or not, at the time it seemed better than anything else I could do.

If, as I claim, the world never causes us to do and feel what we do, I must acknowledge that billions of people, especially those who live their lives in poverty and misery, might bitterly resent this contention. For them, the telephone never rings, the light never turns green, and almost all they have are cacti in which to roll whether they like it or not. Nevertheless, what I will explain is that regardless of our circumstances, all any of us do, think, and feel is always our best attempt *at the time* to satisfy the forces within us. I recognize that there are countless numbers of people whose best efforts do not work; no matter what they are able to do, they are cold, hungry, or brutalized. But I also claim that it does them no good either to accept their misery or to blame it on the world. To do so deprives them of all the opportunities they desperately need to take charge of their lives. Those few of the huge numbers of deprived who do beat the odds and take charge of their lives learn early not to spend much energy blaming the world for their predicaments.

For many of us who are not so desperately situated, taking charge of our lives is much more possible. But even with all of our opportunities, we will never succeed if, for example, we blame our school failure on the teacher or our lack of work on the economy. And the spare tires around our waists are not the fault of Baskin-Robbins; they are because we spend too much time eating mocha fudge ripple. When you learn to put choice theory to work in your life, you will spend your energy attacking the problem—not blaming it. No matter how you get into the cacti, complaining is ineffective; you may as well climb out, patch yourself up, get going, and learn to stay away from those thorns in the future.

2. Replacing External Control With the New Choice Theory Psychology

No one wants to believe that unhappiness can be the underlying cause of so many of their painful and disabling symptoms. Everyone seems to prefer to accept that something physical must be wrong with their brains and that they must be mentally ill. So I teach them something new that few of them have thought about, and then I am able to get through to them. I explain that if they are willing to replace the external control they are now using with a new way of relating called choice theory, they will be much happier. I also say they will be happier if they can learn to escape from the external control someone is using on them. As soon as I mention this to an individual or group, everyone wants to know what external control is.

External control is very simple. In a relationship it is a belief that what we choose to do is right and what the other person does is wrong. The world is filled with external control, and most of us learn it from parents, grandparents, and school teachers—many of whom use it in much of what they do. It was external control that destroyed your marriage if you are divorced, and if you continue to use it in your present relationships, you may be unhappy for the rest of your life. Husbands know what's right for their wives and wives for their husbands. That external-control attitude, *I know what is right for you*, is what people use when they are in unhappy relationships. One or both may use it, but even if only one uses it consistently, it will eventually destroy that relationship. We are social creatures. We need each other. Fritjof Capra said, "All larger organisms, including ourselves, are living testimonies to the fact that destructive practices do not work in the long run. In the end the aggressors always destroy themselves, making way for others who know how to cooperate and get along."[3] Teaching everyone the dangers of external control and how to replace it with choice theory is the heart and soul of encouraging successful and happy lives.

It took thousands of years, but it was as a result of the need for power that all human beings learned to use external control psychology when they can't get along with each other. It comes as a surprise to most of the people we teach that I believe humans have a biological need for power that is unique to us. No other creature has this need. As we evolved, this may have been the last need encoded into our genes and probably came with the onset of civilization. When we began to live near each other in large numbers, we increased competition and our use of power in attempts to control others. Since power can enhance survival in difficult circumstances, it is not necessarily always bad. Driven by power, people have created the many wonders of science, art, and even democracy. People who successfully controlled their lives survived and passed on their power genes to their children. Keep in mind that power is encoded in our genes—external control is not. But if external control gets too involved in a relationship, the relationship is often destroyed.

To begin with a common example, there is a high probability that a large proportion of the married people in the world will remain in dissatisfying marriages or divorce at least once. People going through divorce often have no idea why they have gone from some of the happiest times of their lives to the pain and bitterness of divorce. When I encounter people in this situation, I explain that the solution to this mystery is that too much external control was used in the marriage.

While they are thinking about this idea, I go on to explain that choice theory includes a total of five needs encoded in our genes: survival, love and belonging, freedom, fun, and, of course, power. To be happy we must find ways to satisfy these needs too, but it is the loss of love that is so puzzling to people who divorce.

We are social creatures who need each other. The need for love and belonging is also encoded in our genes. I emphasize the need for love, because to satisfy that need, we have to find another person to love us. This makes love a more difficult need to satisfy than survival, freedom, or fun. After a happy start, many people find that their love has disappeared. For any relationship to last, both partners have to work to keep the love going. If even just one partner chooses to stop using external control, the marriage can begin to improve.

External control is learned, and we can learn through education to replace it with choice theory. To help you learn more about external control, I have grouped together what I call the seven deadly habits of external control that destroy our relationships. We all learned these habits, no matter what part of the world we came from. They are:

- criticizing,
- blaming,
- complaining,
- nagging,
- threatening,
- punishing, and
- bribing or rewarding to control.

There are more than these seven, but if you can stop using these, you will be well on the way to a happy life. You may ask, "What can I replace them with?" I suggest the seven caring habits of choice theory that can improve all relationships:

- supporting,
- encouraging,
- listening,
- accepting,
- trusting,
- respecting,
- and negotiating differences.

I predict that everyone reading this book has had bad experiences with the deadly habits. If you even begin to replace them with a few of the caring habits, especially respect, you will immediately feel a distinct improvement in the quality of your life. Getting rid of the deadly habits in all your relationships is central to leading a happier life.

Choice theory is a new way of thinking and acting more effectively. Choice theory psychology, then, is the exact opposite of external control psychology. Choice theory thinking differs from external control, because when we use choice theory, we assume we are internally motivated to choose behaviors that will help us to get what we want without destroying the relationships we value. Our brains are constantly comparing what we perceive we have with what we really want and need. Based on this comparison, we act in an attempt to balance the two. When what we have matches what we want, we are satisfied, and we usually choose to continue doing whatever we are doing to maintain this balance. But when what we have in reality and what we want inside do not match, the urge to change that situation drives us to choose behaviors that may or may not work. Choice theory illustrates how to evaluate other choices.

We take charge of our own affairs by making the choices to do what works more often than what does not work. We take charge of our lives more effectively by learning why and how we and others behave. Choice theory psychology gives you the tools you need to improve all your relationships and create a life for yourself that is what you want it to be. When you know choice theory, you will never again be controlled by forces outside yourself unless you choose to be. With choice theory, you can understand why attempting to control others is impossible to accomplish without destroying your relationships with them. When you learn choice theory, you will understand that the only person you can control is yourself.

As you learn to get external control out of your life, you will begin to notice a few people around you who are very different from a lot of people you know because they seem to be happy most of the time. If you get to know them, you will soon notice that they are not controlling. They don't try to change anyone. They have learned to live and let live. If people try to control them, they will have learned a variety of ways to escape that control. These are people you will want to get to know.

3. The Pictures in Our Heads

like to think that all our senses combine into an extraordinary camera that can take visual pictures, auditory pictures, gustatory pictures, tactile pictures, and so forth. In simple terms, this sensory camera can take a picture of anything we can perceive through any of our senses. I like to use the word *pictures* rather than the technically correct term *perceptions*, because pictures are easier to understand. Our memory is capable of sorting and storing the vast numbers of pictures that enter our senses each day. My clinical observation is that we learn some pictures are more important to us than others, and we place these important pictures in a special place in our memory. I call this place the quality world. Since more than 80 percent of the perceptions we store in our quality worlds are visual, *pictures* is a reasonably accurate term.

Suppose you had a grandson, and your daughter left you in charge while he was taking a nap. She said she would be right back because he would be ravenous when he woke, and she knew you had no idea what to feed an eleven-month-old child. She was right. As soon as she left, he woke up screaming furiously, obviously starving. You tried a chocolate-chip cookie, and it worked wonders. At first, he did not seem to know what it was, but he was a quick learner. He quickly polished off three cookies. She returned and almost polished you off for being so stupid as to give a baby chocolate. "Now," she said, "he will be yelling all day for those cookies." She was right. If he is like most of us, he will probably have chocolate on his mind for the rest of his life. I'm sure grandparents reading this will sympathize. After all, what is our purpose, if not for introducing grandchildren to the finer things in life?

I tell this story to illustrate how we develop the pictures in our heads—the specific pictures that we believe will satisfy our built-in needs. Based on our biological nature, I believe that at the time we are conceived, the requirement that we satisfy our basic needs is built into our genetic instructions; but when we are born, we have not the slightest idea of what these needs are or how to fulfill them. To satisfy them, even before birth we begin to create the quality world from our perceptions and ideas and begin to fill it with detailed pictures of what we want. Our whole lives will be spent enlarging the selection of pictures in our quality worlds. Dan Gilbert, professor of psychology at Harvard University, has written a popular review of research on perception. He says "The greatest achievement of the human brain is its ability to imagine objects and episodes that do not exist in the realm of the real, and it is this ability that allows us to think about the future."[4]

The baby in the above story has begun to understand that when he wakes up, the urge he feels is hunger. He also knows, when he looks through his small quality world, that the picture of his bottle is not what he wants to satisfy his hunger. I doubt that he has the picture of any specific food in his tiny quality world, and I am sure that he knows nothing about chocolate-chip cookies, but he has the hazy picture of something that is not the bottle.

He also knows how to cry. He learned to cry moments after he was born and has been crying ever since with great success to get his urges satisfied. Well aware that when he cries, people start moving to pacify him, he uses this behavior to control others, including his grandfather. To those of us who have long had a picture of chocolate-chip cookies and a thousand other delicious foods in our quality worlds, this all seems quite simple. But for the baby, it is far from simple to find out what will satisfy the urges he feels when, in the beginning, he hardly knows what these urges are.

It is like going to the store and telling the clerk that you want something—"Please bring it quickly." When he asks you what it is, you say, "Something that will satisfy me, you fool, and bring it right away!" He is a willing clerk, and he brings you one item after another, but you keep yelling that he is a miserable incompetent and he should please hurry up and get what you want or you will take the store apart.

We've all been in that clerk's position with babies, animals, and even plants: if a favorite plant starts to die, we say, "If only I knew what it wants." But when we start out, none of us knows what we want; we only know we desperately want something—so we may scream, cry, pout, or thrash about randomly to try to get it. When what we do gets us something that satisfies a need, we store the picture of what satisfied us in a place in our heads. This is how we learn what we want. When that baby learned how satisfying chocolate-chip cookies were, he pasted the picture of those cookies in his quality world, where it's my guess he will keep it for the rest of his life.

He was crying to get the world to offer him something to satisfy his hunger. Although he did not know what would do it, he was able to master the simple logic that if he didn't have it, it must be outside himself. This means that to recognize whatever it was, he had to make contact with the world. The way all living creatures make this contact is through the senses associated with our eyes, ears, fingers, tongues, and noses. But it is also important to keep in mind that it is through these same senses that we make contact with our own minds and bodies, both of which are, to us, a very important part of the real world.

After biting into the cookie, the baby liked it very much. Immediately, he took a picture of that cookie with his sensory camera and stored it in his quality world as a picture of something to look for again when he got a similar urge. He might not yet have completely understood that the urge was hunger, but what he did know was that, whatever it was, chocolate-chip cookies satisfied it.

This means that we store in our quality worlds the pictures of anything in the real world that we believe will satisfy one or more of our basic needs. For the rest of his life, when that baby gets hungry, he will start tuning in to his quality world. Many times, when he comes to the pictures of chocolate-chip cookies, he will say to himself, "That's what I want right now," and he'll try to find a chocolate-chip cookie in the real world. I have some friends who tell me that there are times, especially when they are on diets, that they think they could kill for chocolate. With a little thought, it will become apparent that your quality world (the pictures in your head) is the specific motivation for all you attempt to do with your life.

Everything you know, however, is not stored in your quality world—it is not the same as your memory. For example, to satisfy our needs, we speak and read, and to do this we store all the words we use and recognize in our memories, but these words are not in our quality worlds unless they are part of a need-satisfying picture. It satisfies many people to say grace before meals, so prayer is in their quality worlds, but the specific words that make up that prayer are stored in their larger memories. The quality world in my head is a small, selective part of my total memory. It is the world that I want right now—it could even be called my ideal world, but it is more than ideal; it is the world I believe I must have or my needs will not be satisfied. That is why I call it the quality world.

Our personal quality worlds are never hazy or general; they always contain very specific pictures of what will satisfy our needs right now. Anything that satisfies me, I store. If I see something that does not fulfill any part of any need, I will pay little or no attention to it. I may, of course, be aware that something is there, and I may even know what it is; for example, I still remember that I had a green Chevrolet in 1950. But that picture, while it may be in my memory, is no longer in my quality world, as it does not presently satisfy any need.

While I am making up my mind whether a picture satisfies me, I may store it in my quality world temporarily, but if it does not pass the test of being something worth keeping, I will remove it. This is why old people who are feeble and can no longer actively fulfill their never-ceasing needs have little memory for the present. What is the sense of storing what is unsatisfying? For the past, however, when they were capable of dealing effectively with the world, their memory is excellent. As we grow older and less effective, we tend to paste fewer and fewer pictures into our quality worlds. To maintain our self-esteem, we want to talk about the good old pictures, the ones we pasted in permanently when we were young and effective.

When a picture that has been in my quality world for years is no longer as satisfying as I would like it to be, I will often look for a new, more satisfying picture to replace it. It is like my old car: I replaced it with a better new one. This is what a man named Dave did when he left his wife for another woman. He had Susan in his quality world for many years as a need-satisfying wife. Then, for reasons known only to him that he may never choose to share with anyone, he replaced her with the picture of someone else. It may be that the new woman better satisfied his need for love. If she was wealthy, she may have satisfied a long-frustrated need for power, or if she was more tolerant of his lifestyle, she may have satisfied his need for freedom. For whatever reason, maybe even for fun, he put her picture in and took Susan's out. And when we change important pictures, we change our lives.

It is likely that we have hundreds and even thousands of pictures that will satisfy each need. If we come from large, loving families, we may have a hundred relatives that we like to be with—but ...

We must have at least one picture for every need.

If we have no picture at all, the need that is unsatisfied will drive us first to look for a picture that may satisfy it and then for a way to make satisfying contact with whatever it is in the real world that the picture represents. To have a need without quickly finding a picture to satisfy it is almost impossible. But keep in mind that we commonly have pictures in our quality worlds that cannot be satisfied in the real world—if wishes were horses, then beggars would ride.

Another man I talked to who attempted suicide said he had no one, and he despaired of ever finding someone. In his despair he attempted to kill himself; life without a picture to satisfy the need to belong is really a life without hope. My guess is that he did have someone, but because he could not make a connection with that person, he was so hopeless that he said he had no one. The problem is rarely that there are no pictures; more often, we can't satisfy the pictures we have. Unless we are genetically flawed—as are sociopaths, who seem to have a strong need for power but no need to belong—we usually have at least one picture of someone we want to love in our quality worlds at all times.

The power of the pictures in our quality world is huge. In our relentless efforts to satisfy them, we may go so far as to choose behaviors that endanger our lives rather than change our cherished pictures. For centuries parents have become distraught when a teenage daughter chooses to stop eating and begins to starve to death. It is called by its ancient Latin label, anorexia nervosa—loss of appetite for no known physical reason. Some understanding of this crazy choice not to eat can be gleaned through the concept of the pictures in our heads. A researcher who did an ingenious experiment with anorexics showed them pictures depicting their heads superimposed on a series of bodies ranging from what most of us would call normal all the way to skeletal. Then he asked the young women, "Which of the bodies do you like seeing your head attached to?" To the researcher's surprise, they said none of them—all were too fat. What they were saying was that they wanted to be thinner than whatever they saw in the mirror. To achieve this irrational degree of thinness, they had no choice but to starve themselves, and they did.

This example illustrates that the pictures in our quality worlds do not have to be rational. Crazy or sane, all any picture has to do is fulfill the need that the person decides is most important at the time. Although this does not explain why an anorexic pastes in that life-endangering picture, it does lead any sensible physician treating her to tell her that he will not allow her to starve herself to death. If necessary, she will be force-fed to keep her alive. Because anorexics aim to be thinner but not to die, this treatment makes some sense, and more importantly, it keeps them alive while a good counselor can provide the support they need to choose to change the pictures in their quality worlds. Once they make the extremely difficult choice to change their pictures, they are horrified that they are so thin, and they start to eat. Later, we will talk about how this is done.

Alcoholics are dominated by the picture of themselves satisfying any and all of their needs through alcohol. As long as this wonderful, all-satisfying picture is in their quality worlds, they will drink not only when they are frustrated but also to prevent possible future frustration. Any therapy that does not change the picture of alcohol satisfying their needs to something less destructive will be ineffective. When they join Alcoholics Anonymous, as many do, they begin to replace the picture of alcohol with AA. If they attend AA regularly, they are able to stop drinking, because being involved with this satisfying organization keeps the picture of AA predominant. All alcoholics who are AA regulars believe that the picture of them drinking alcohol is never completely removed from their quality worlds. It may be moved far to the back, but not out. They contend—and they should know—that if they fail to attend AA and do not keep the AA picture large and active in the front of their quality worlds, they will slip back to drinking.

Sexuality, especially homosexuality, can be a very controversial subject, because there are a lot of different ideas about it. From my experience in counseling, I have learned that an approach to sexuality based on choice theory is very practical, because choice theory focuses on improving relationships. For reasons that no one can yet explain, when we get any sexually satisfying picture, conventional or unconventional, into our quality world, this picture is almost impossible to remove. If we can't change the pictures ourselves—and there is, as yet, no counseling technique that can lead us to change most of them—then we must accept the pictures we have. Difficult as this may be, we must learn as well as we can to live with them within the rules of society. If we attempt to engage in any long-term sexual activity that is different from the pictures in our heads because of cultural pressure, we will be either unable or unwilling to perform sexually. To some extent, the idea of quality world pictures can explain why homosexuals and others find it impossible to change their pictures.

The pictures in your quality world represent the specific life you want to live. And if this life involves real people who may not want to play the exact part in your life that you assign to them in your quality world, you may engage in a long, miserable struggle to get them to change. Susan is now engaged in this struggle, because Dave refuses to be what she wants him to be. If he won't go back to what she wants—and it is likely he won't—her choice is either to continue her losing battle or to replace his picture. Fortunately, the picture of whom we love is usually replaceable with someone else, and my guess is that eventually Susan will do this.

Large-brained humans are more capable of changing their pictures than lower creatures, but at any one time, we want what we want and nothing else. I eat my eggs over hard, because that is the picture in my head of how eggs should be eaten. My late wife would shudder as she cooked them, because that was not the picture in her head. When she urged me to eat my eggs softer, she had no chance of succeeding unless she could persuade me to change my picture. It is likely that before he left, Dave had many arguments with Susan over the different pictures of marriage each had in his and her quality worlds. Husbands, wives, and families that do not get along together always have vastly different pictures in their heads of how each wants to be satisfied by the other.

It is not easy to change our own pictures, but it is even more difficult to persuade others to change theirs. To change a picture, we have to replace it with another that is at least reasonably satisfying. *This can be done only through negotiation and compromise; force will not work.*

Most people do not know that they are motivated by the pictures in their heads and have no idea how powerful and specific they are. In most relationships, even good ones, we constantly attempt to force others to change to what we want. Try to force your son to play little-league baseball, your daughter to cut her waist-long hair, your husband to play bridge, or your wife to jog five miles before breakfast, and you risk a hornets' nest of resistance. Think how hard it is for you to throw out a favorite old sweater now in tatters, a relatively insignificant thing, and you begin to see how quickly you *strongly resent* anyone who pressures you to change a picture.

People who live together must learn that it is impossible for any two of us to have the same pictures in our heads. Expand this to a family, and the odds against perfectly shared pictures grow even greater. No two people can live exactly the same life, and though we are all driven by the same needs, even these needs usually vary in strength from person to person. I may need love much more than you do, and you may be more driven by power than I am. But both of us need some of both, and our success as a couple will depend on how well we can agree on some specific pictures that will satisfy these needs. If you and I live together and share half the pictures in our quality worlds, we probably have more in common than most. If we want to satisfy the need to belong, which drives us together, we must learn to share what we have in common and accept—or at least tolerate—the pictures we don't share.

If we want to take charge of our lives, the knowledge that no two of us can share all the same pictures must become an integral part of the way we deal with those around us.

Tim, your teenage son, refuses to work in school, listens to what you think is weird music all night long, and admits to smoking marijuana. You and he have different pictures of what life should be. It seems to you that it is impossible to talk to him about anything—just looking at him makes you upset. Variations on this theme run through all families. When the pictures get to be impossibly different in a marriage, a divorce is possible, but you can't divorce a child or a parent. It's even hard to separate completely from a brother or sister. Frustrating as they may be, they are not easy to replace.

In our attempts to patch up failing relationships, we usually try to force a change. We pressure Tim to work in school and stop smoking pot. We take away the car, cut his allowance, restrict his friends from the house, and impose a curfew. But this rarely works. Whether you like it or not, Tim may even rub it in by saying, "Look,

I don't hassle you, why don't you leave me alone?" And you always rise to the bait with a lecture that you are not nagging him, only trying to point out how he is ruining his life. As you do, things between the two of you continue to deteriorate. Still, you nag because you can't accept Tim's attitude toward school or his use of drugs no matter how hard you try. The way he chooses to live his life is incompatible with your picture of how you think he should behave.

To get along with Tim and perhaps eventually persuade him to change some of his pictures, you need to start the process by trying to find some pictures that you and Tim still share. One shared picture will get the process started. The only way any relationship can be patched up when the pictures are very different is to try to find one or more new pictures that can be shared or to try again to share some old ones that once satisfied you both. You must look for something that you and Tim can do together, something you both want to do, and then do it. Let's suppose that at one time you enjoyed fishing with Tim, but for a long time you have been getting along so badly that you haven't even considered asking him to go fishing. You now realize that you must find a satisfying way to get together, so you offer to take him fishing, saying, "Just fishing, no lectures." He accepts, you do it, and the two of you get along well for a weekend. It's a little like old times. If you are patient, don't lecture, and do a few more things together that work, you have a chance to patch up any once-strong relationship. If what Tim is choosing to do with his life is not need fulfilling in the long run, and it usually is not, he may begin to pay attention to what you have been saying. Remember, you have already said what you think many times; you don't have to keep on saying it.

With many children, parents, brothers, or sisters, this may be all we can do. We may have to settle for what we can share and accept that many of the pictures in our quality worlds will never be the same, but:

The better we get along, the more pictures we will begin to share again.

If you kick Tim out of the house in frustration, all you are likely to accomplish is losing him. But your concern is that if you do nothing, he may destroy himself before your eyes. This is a tough dilemma with no easy solutions, but if you keep in mind that you must find some pictures to share, you will realize that you can't accomplish this if you kick him out. A compromise might be to try a middle course—let him stay, but set rules for no loud music and no pot smoking in the house as minimal conditions. If he breaks these rules, tell him he has to leave for twelve hours and come back and try again. Continue to talk to him pleasantly (no lectures) and try to share at least one pleasurable activity with him each week, but offer no money or other tangible support unless he goes to school or work. Then wait and wait.

Persuading someone to change pictures always takes a long time. Don't look for anyone to prescribe the exact path to follow between toughness and laxness. It does not exist. But if you stay close to Tim through keeping good contact at home and with an occasional fishing trip, the path widens. He has more choices than the limited ones of destroying himself at home or leaving with little ability to take care of himself on his own.

If we want to stay with others, we must spend our time enjoying what we do share, always trying to find new pictures to share, and accepting or at least tolerating what is not shared. If you find that you just can't accept a different picture in your wife's quality world, perhaps you can work out an agreement that today you'll do it your way and tomorrow you'll do it hers. Many people work out vacations that way. If you are in the middle of a deteriorating relationship right now, you should take the initiative to try to work out some compatible pictures with your partner. Don't wait for him to do this; he doesn't know how. Even if only one of you understands the importance of the pictures in your heads, you have a better chance of getting along together.

The new pictures we put in our heads often conflict with old ones. Dave may have a picture of himself as a very loyal person and feels miserably disloyal as he tries to find a better life with his new wife. But if he were to return to Susan, there might still be insufficient love, fun, or freedom to satisfy other pictures that are important to him. Later in this book, I will explain conflict in great detail, but for now it is important that you understand that there is nothing in choice theory that says the pictures in our heads have to be compatible. In fact, incompatibility and even conflict are common in all our quality worlds. Dave's picture of himself as loyal will not disappear just because he has met a new and, to him, exciting woman. It may put a damper on this new relationship for years. To continue to see himself as loyal, he might act in a financially responsible way toward Susan, so at least to that extent she might benefit from that picture.

The only way we can take pictures out of our quality worlds is to replace them with others that fulfill the same basic needs reasonably well. Because they can't replace pictures, people will endure a great deal of pain and sometimes choose a lifetime of misery. Many women endure brutal beatings and humiliations in marriage but stay with their husbands because they are still the only possible pictures of a loving person. After suffering abuse, these women may complain that their lives are living hells, but they still stay because they do not believe they can replace their husbands in their quality worlds. If these women could understand the concept of the quality world they would find an answer to the question they continually ask themselves: "Why do I stay?" They might seek a better picture more actively and begin to take charge of their lives.

But what if we are deprived of the way we have fulfilled a need for years? Suppose a beloved spouse dies—what happens to that picture? For a while, nothing happens. It remains the same as always; in fact, sometime it gets a little better as we tend to glorify the dead. In the real world we have lost a loved one, but in our quality world, she is still very much alive. This is why we choose to suffer so much when we lose someone. As I will explain later, when there is nothing we can do, we almost always choose to suffer. But grieving is also sensible. Those close to us gather around, and we are reassured that many still care. In time, we accept that we cannot bring the loved one back to life. Supported by friends and relatives, we begin the slow, painful process of removing her from our present pictures, realizing that to keep her there would cause us to grieve forever.

Although it is never possible to deny the pictures in our quality worlds, at times we still try to push them out of mind, because to admit that we can do nothing to achieve them is painful. We all have pictures in our quality worlds of how our marriages could be better or our jobs more rewarding, but we try to deny these pictures, because to admit their existence opens up wounds we would rather keep closed. We try to tell ourselves everything is fine, but we are still unsatisfied.

A lonely woman once came to me for counseling and said that the previous day she had gone to an emergency room because she could hardly breathe. She was still short of breath. The doctors had not been able to find much wrong except that she smoked too much. Gasping as she spoke, she vehemently denied that her shortness of breath might be psychological. But as we talked about what she wanted, which was a good relationship, and as she began to feel that with my help she might learn to find one, her breathing eased. She found it hard to admit that she needed help; her shortness of breath became her way to ask for it.

Your quality world—in which you find love, worth, success, fun, and freedom—is the world you would like to live in, where somehow or other all desires, even conflicting ones, are satisfied. None of us has a picture in our quality world of doing badly ourselves. We may at times choose to do what those around us say is self-destructive, but we don't do these things to destroy ourselves. The pictures we are trying to satisfy make sense to us. Tim did not think he was destroying his life; his father did.

Sometimes we may choose to fail (in the mind of someone else—a father, for example) because it seems to us that this failure will get us more of what we want than if we succeed. To Tim, success in school might set the stage for a career, such as law, that he does not want. Less specifically, to succeed might be to put himself in the position for his father to make greater and greater demands that take Tim farther and farther from the pictures in his head. None of us wants to fail, but we must keep in mind that no two of us have the same picture of success. It is the picture of success in *your* head, nobody else's, that causes you to do what you do.

4. Our Values-Driven Behaviors

"Beauty is in the eye of the beholder," and so, of course, are ugliness, genius, greatness, and meanness. All our values, good and bad, come from within ourselves. In the real world, where everything exists, there are no values, labels, or designations of any kind. In order to communicate sensibly, as language developed we began to agree on what to call the many objects we encountered. Over many years, in a variety of languages, a tree became a tree, up became up, and sweet, sweet, until all we knew about had one or more descriptive designations.

As long as we were describing a particular configuration like a man or a river, we could usually agree. But later—to warn others about someone who might harm them or to tell about a crystal-clear river—we began to add values to our descriptions. We talked about a bad man or a good river, but when we did, we often disagreed vehemently, and this disagreement over values is still very much with us. It is almost impossible to avoid discussing values, because by now we have evolved to the point where our sensory cameras add either a good or bad value to almost every significant thing we perceive. Unless we consciously intervene, this happens quickly, automatically, and without any awareness on our part that we are doing it. Values seem to be as much a part of what we see as color, shape, or size; but unlike these more descriptive labels, they are much more personal. For example, although few of us argue about a person's skin color, we do argue about the value of the person whose skin is that color.

With good intent, I once told a friend not to encourage his son to act so stupidly, and it took five years to reestablish the friendship. I did this quickly and without thinking, because when I said it, the boy was doing something so patently foolish, in my view, that I could not imagine his father could think otherwise. In choice theory terms, I have a picture in my head of how kids should behave, and when I saw my friend's son behaving so differently from that picture, I called his behavior stupid before I could stop myself. The reason I could not stop myself was that it did not seem to me that I first saw the boy and then added the adjective *stupid*. What I saw through my sensory camera was one picture—stupid boy.

How many people did you pin a value on yesterday with no awareness on your part that you were doing it? As you drove to work, didn't you hear some fool on the radio claiming you could lose weight and still eat all you wanted? And no matter how many times you have given instructions, didn't your lazy secretary fail to open and sort your mail? Did your close-minded boss refuse for the fifth time to listen to your great plan to reorganize your department? Upon arriving home after a grueling day, didn't you see that your good-for-nothing son had failed to mow the lawn and set out the trash? And did your high-school-senior daughter, who obviously doesn't know right from wrong, hit you with her harebrained plan to hitchhike through Europe all summer with a boy she hardly knows? Didn't it seem to you, as you encountered these people behaving so differently from the pictures in your quality world, that *close-minded, lazy, good-for-nothing,* and *harebrained* were as much attached to those people as their arms and legs?

But those values have not always been attached to your son, daughter, boss, and secretary. For years, your son was a good kid struggling to find himself, and until the sudden advent of the hitchhike scheme, your daughter was your darling who could do no wrong. Even your secretary was a hard worker until recently, when personal problems began to occupy so much of her time that she could not keep her mind on her work. And for years, until he started to be harassed by a power-mad vice president, your understanding boss took time to listen to all your suggestions.

If you want to take charge of your life, you must become aware that your sensory camera is no ordinary camera faithfully recording the world as it is. It is an extraordinary camera that pictures the world as you would like it to be. The way you want to see the world is as close as possible to the pictures in your head. Therefore, to fulfill your need for love, for a few years you saw your unemployed son as struggling to find himself. To have seen him otherwise would have been frustrating. Thousands of European artists painted Christ not as the dark Middle Easterner that he was but as the fair-skinned Nordic man of the picture in their heads.

When what we see has little to do with what we want, our cameras record reality quite faithfully. For example, when I am working inside, I see a gray, windy day as just that; the weather is unimportant. But on my day off, when I want to play tennis, the same day is a perfect day for a game. This is why our friends tell us frequently to face reality. It is easier for them to see today as it is, because the reality does not frustrate them. My wife, who does not play tennis, often says with great accuracy, "How can you consider playing on such a rotten day?" But I want to play so badly that my sensory camera steps in and does its best to improve the weather.

Even the most obedient sensory cameras, however, have limits as to how much they can distort the world. Much as we want to live the pictures in our heads, we must live in the real world, where a son's two years' sitting home no longer fulfills our needs. As it does not, we slowly begin to see him more as he is and less as we hope him to be. Finally, in an effort to regain control (because hoping is a very ineffective behavior), we begin to pin the label *good-for-nothing* or *vegetating* on him, just as yesterday we called our secretary lazy, the boss close-minded, and daughter harebrained.

Our frustration drives us to make this change in values when kindness, patience, and tolerance seem not to get us what we want. Pushed by our ever-present need for power, we begin to think, "If he won't change, I will change him." But before we act, we want to define the difference between what is right (the pictures in our heads) and what is wrong (how he is acting) as sharply as possible.

Labels like lazy, close-minded, or good-for-nothing quickly make this difference clear and help us to justify whatever we choose to do to get him to see the light. We may righteously kick this good-for-nothing son out. We may also consider cutting off our harebrained daughter's allowance, lecturing our lazy secretary, and even sabotaging our close-minded boss—all in the attempt to get them to change. If we have any doubts about the wisdom of what we are doing, our own labels reduce these doubts. To gain support for what we have done or plan to do, we talk to friends and family about these problems, always using the labels to help convince them we are right. After all, who would argue that we ought to extend our patience beyond two years with a son who sits and vegetates?

It is very likely that values became part of the way we saw the world early in our evolution. Those who could see dangers had a clear survival advantage over those who stopped to figure out what was going on. For example, when our ancestors came face-to-face with a saber-toothed tiger, they had to be able to look at him, see he was dangerous, and act immediately. We are not descended from people who stopped and thought things over in this situation. Today we teach our children to see a gun or a stranger as dangerous, not to wait and make this determination for themselves. Many guns and most strangers are not dangerous, but enough of them are that we believe it is a good idea that we teach our children to see guns and strangers this way.

When we assign values to those we love, these values can cause a great deal of frustration. There's no problem with good values, such as loving, hardworking, or generous, but when you fall into the trap of seeing your son as good-for-nothing, the gap between the two of you widens every time you look at him or think of him. If your son reforms, as many good-for-nothings do, it may take a long time to adapt to his new behavior because of the way you saw him for so long. You would have been better off if you had never pinned this label on him.

Once a value is in our cameras, we tend to use it. To avoid frustration, we should make a continuing effort to remain aware that we put the value there and we can take it out. If, as a small child, you put the value that strangers are dangerous into your camera, you may be uneasy with people unless you've known them for years. Long after any rational danger from them has passed, you may still be ill at ease because the value remains in your camera.

Just as we can gain a great deal of control by learning that we choose to depress ourselves and that better choices are available, we must learn that far too often we choose to add labels to what we see.

One of the most difficult lessons to master as we struggle to create effective change is to learn not to label something as bad just because it is different from what we want.

It is much easier to satisfy our needs in a different world than a bad one. The fewer bad values we attach to what we see, the more effective we will be.

For example, take an imaginary walk with me around my neighborhood. Immediately I see my next-door neighbor's lawn cluttered with a pile of junk. It is not easy to get along with a neighbor who has a junkyard for a front lawn. Then I see a disreputable bum cruising in my neighborhood in an old, beat-up truck. He becomes a burglar looking for a house to rob, and my heart starts an unhealthy pounding.

It is as if we have two stockpiles of labels—one good, the other bad—stored in the back of our cameras. As soon as we see anything that significantly differs from what we want, without any awareness we attach a label from the bad stockpile and see it as bad. If what we see coincides with what we want, a good label is instantly added to the picture in the same way.

Good values present few problems, but bad labels cause us a great deal of difficulty—because as we add them, we increase the difference between what we see and what we want, and the larger this difference becomes, the more we must act to reduce it. Too many bad labels will lead us to exhaust ourselves in unproductive arguing, fighting, rejecting, backbiting, gossiping, moralizing, preaching, and conspiring. For example, calling a son good-for-nothing or a daughter harebrained may give us a temporary sense of superiority. But they also lead us to argue, fight, or depress—hardly effective ways to get them to be the children we want them to be. We all know this, but we seem unable to stop, because we fail to realize that the source of our ineffective behavior is as much our labels as it is their behavior.

Tolerance, a virtue more professed than practiced, means making an effort to accept that others, even those we love, have different pictures in their heads. Probably so many of us are intolerant because once we choose to pin a bad value on someone, our own action increases the difference beyond what we can accept. To be tolerant, we must learn how quickly we add bad values, and we must make an effort to recognize that this need not be automatic. We can say to ourselves, "What good does it do to call my son good-for-nothing? How will this help me to persuade him that he has to do more than sit around? If he needs my help, how will he get it if I call him bad names, fight with him, or depress?" Whenever we see someone as bad, we must stop and ask ourselves, "Will this label help me get what I want?" If the answer is no, we should try to remove the label. The less we label, the more we will be in charge of our lives.

At the back of our sensory cameras, behind the stockpiles of values, all of us have valuing filters, and we use them to classify perceptions as positive, negative, or neutral. For example, people who admire fashion as a personal value system look at the world through the fashion filter. Anything in style is seen as good; what is not is seen as bad. Fashion predominates in all they do. If they play tennis, the style of their apparel may be more important than how well they hit the ball.

Many people have a money filter in their camera and view all they see in terms of what it costs. If they are economical, cheap is good and expensive is bad. If they are status-conscious or anxious to impress with wealth, expensive is good and cheap is bad. A rose has more beauty if it is a rare, expensive variety. A sunset is more glorious if it is viewed from the veranda at St. Martinique. The people with whom they associate are clever or attractive in proportion to their wealth: they filter their lives through their bank accounts. Fashion and money are good examples of the many personal value systems that color our lives.

When most of us think of value systems, what first comes to our minds are universal systems of belief, such as religion and politics. Fundamentalists filter all they see through their religious teachings: what supports the written word of God is good. Chicago Democrats may see all the machine does as good and anything opposed to it as not good. American Civil Liberties Union members see the world as good or bad depending on whether or not personal freedom is advanced. Many conservatives see small government as good and liberal ideas as bad.

Many organizations also have a code of values: companies like Microsoft encourage their employees to see the world through the company's eyes. Charlie Wilson's famous remark, "What is good for the country is good for General Motors, and vice versa," is a classic example of how the values of a company can dominate the lives of its executives. Lodges like the Masons, unions like the United Auto Workers, professions like law and medicine, and cults like Hare Krishna are just a few of the organizations that provide value systems through which many of those who belong filter what they see.

In our sensory cameras we may have a whole series of filters, each representing a different value system. For the most part, these do not conflict. For example, fashion usually supports politics; it is the rare politician who does not dress with conservative sincerity and have hair that is fashionably styled and blown dry. Occasionally, however, filters may conflict. For example, patriots who also believe strongly in civil liberties may at times have difficulty reconciling their country's actions with the belief that it is always right. Conflict in value systems is infrequent, however, because the purpose of value systems is to help us reduce conflict as we attempt to fulfill our often conflicting needs.

If instead of using value systems we attempt to make a separate evaluation of each component of an important situation, we can't help but run into a great deal of conflict. For example, a good friend is now drinking far too much and is probably already an alcoholic. Looking at each component separately, I see alcoholism as bad, but my friend is good. These values are opposed, and I am in conflict as to whether to keep seeing him or not. If, however, I have a system that values all friends as good no matter what they do, I have no conflict. Following this system, I stick to him through bout after bout of drinking with little discomfort, because my friendship filter removes my concern over his drinking. Conversely, if my value system holds that all alcoholics are no good, friends or not, I can tell him that until he stops drinking, he and I are through. Of course, as much as these value systems may help me, they do little for my friend—he needs my friendship, not my acceptance or rejection.

Therefore, while a value system may work for me to prevent conflict, it is often detrimental to people I need and may eventually frustrate my ability to get along with them. If my company, whose value system I fully endorse, orders me to relocate, I may be deaf to the legitimate complaints of my children who don't want to move. Even those who torture and murder for religious or political beliefs— common crimes throughout history—filter away any conflict they feel by pointing to a higher value system to justify what they do. These people use duty, patriotism, and religion for power and ride roughshod over those who disagree with them.

But value systems also help us to get along with others. Members of organized churches feel the power of God behind them and gain kinship with those who believe as they do. Vegetarians gain the power of good health and the camaraderie of others who shun meat. No matter how personal and obscure the value system, it almost always gives its adherents a feeling of power and a sense of belonging. But the more we adhere to any system, the more this belonging will be limited to others who believe as we do. We may even see our children as bad if they don't follow our way. By excluding others, any rigid system we embrace may frustrate our need to belong.

To reduce this frustration, those who believe in a system almost always proselytize for their beliefs. They feel a loss of control when they see people, especially those who seem to be in good control of their lives, following a different system. But even this they seem able to accept—these people at least have a sense of values. What bothers them most are people who seem free of any system and still get along well.

The most serious and often fatal flaw in any value system is that value systems are always destructive of our need to be free. Whatever freedom any system allows is only available within it. I have several close associates who were, for years, members of an established religious order. They finally left not because they stopped believing but because they could not abide the restrictions on personal freedom demanded by the system. Because we need to be free, the more a value system dominates our lives, the less likely it is that this system will work for a lifetime. Satisfying our often conflicting needs requires creativity, which is always variable and unpredictable—only a noncreative machine can follow a system forever.

Although it takes more effort, you will be more in charge of your life if you evaluate each situation as you encounter it rather than relying too much on any one value system. If our children join a dangerous gang, most of us adhere to value systems that lead us quickly to consider rejecting those children. But if we can refrain from viewing their move through such a system, we will be less inclined to do what will separate us even more from our children. We must keep in mind that children join restrictive organizations because they are searching for a set of values that will give them more control over their lives. If we reject them, causing a further loss of control, they will cling more tightly to the group they have joined.

If you are not restrained to follow an anti-gang value system, you will find it easier to keep in touch, because you may be able to see only the *move* as bad, not the child. You must, however, be cautious not to criticize the gang members, because your child now has the gang's beliefs as the major filter in his camera. If your child tries to get you to understand, let him talk and don't argue. He is as much trying to convince himself as you; and if you argue, he will work harder, and may even convince himself. When we label someone bad, we have more trouble dealing with that person than if we could have settled for a lesser label. We tend to anger much more at a bad child than at a slow or careless child, because the difference between the picture of the child you want and a bad child is greater than the difference between your picture and a slow or careless child. The greater the difference between the pictures, the greater the pressure to behave, and under pressure we are less likely to find an effective behavior.

The fewer value systems we have in our cameras, the less we will label what we see, and the less we will be pressured to act. With less pressure, we will have the time to figure out flexible and creative behaviors that may be more effective. We must recognize that we embrace value systems not only because they seem to work at the time but because they promise to work forever to satisfy our needs. Few, if any, systems consistently deliver on this promise. When they fail, as they almost always will, it is important to realize that much of our current problem may be in how our value systems have distorted what we see. Seen without these systems, the world is much easier to deal with.

5. Why We Behave

The best way to begin the explanation of why we behave is to take a look at how a thermostat controls the air temperature in a room. Most of us don't realize that a thermostat is not activated by cold or hot air—what activates it is the difference between the actual temperature and the desired temperature. In much the same way, Susan chose to be upset as her best effort to deal with the difference between the desired picture of Dave in her head—living with her as her husband—and the picture of Dave in the real world—gone with another woman. Why she chose this way of dealing with this difficult situation, I will explain in later chapters, but first I must explain the cause of all our behaviors—everything that we do, think, or feel.

The thermostat also has an internal world—simple, I'll admit, but still a very specific picture that will not be satisfied until the air around it is at its set temperature. It also has a sensory apparatus, a sensory camera, which can detect whether the temperature in the room is below or above its setting. Then, like us, it can act to reduce that difference. But unlike us, if it can't get the temperature it wants through the furnace or air cooler, it's stuck. There is nothing more that it, a dead machine, can do. Living creatures are never stuck. If we can't get what we want with what we know, we will create new behaviors that may be more effective. But old or new, all our behaviors are a constant attempt to reduce the difference between what we want (the pictures in our heads) and what we have (the way we see situations in the world).

The new behaviors we create may not work. They may be no better or may even be worse in practice than what we have. But there is always the possibility that they will be better, and when we are desperate to get what we want, we will always consider them and often try them. Everything wonderfully innovative from the wheel to the computer has been achieved by people struggling to create something in the real world that was first represented by a picture in their heads. But as I will explain in detail later, everything miserably innovative from heart disease to psychosis has also been created by people involved in this same struggle.

If Dave's wife won't take Dave out of her quality world, she will try to get him back by doing all she knows and all she can learn. She will also consider seriously any new idea that may come to her. She was probably doing something new just by baring her soul to casual acquaintances like my wife. If these attempts fail, as they often do, she cannot quit. Pushed by the picture she wants, she will expand her efforts, and in doing so, she will almost always choose increasingly painful and senseless ways to behave. Whenever there is a difference between what we want and what we have, we must behave—which means acting, thinking, feeling, or involving our body, all of which are components of the total behaviors we generate as we struggle to get what we want.

Take a moment and look back into your own life to a time when you were very frustrated, a time when the picture in your head was far better than the real situation. Didn't you stubbornly hold on to this picture even though the longer you did, the further you got from what you wanted? Didn't you *do* fewer effective things, *think* more irrational thoughts, and *feel* a variety of painful feelings that you may never have felt before? Didn't you approach acquaintances and pour out your tale of woe, driven in this frustrating situation to try a variety of actions, thoughts, and feelings that were to some degree new to you? Did you perhaps think some genuinely crazy thoughts or feel more depressed than ever before? Maybe you got sick or began to act irresponsibly. Perhaps you began to use drugs or alcohol in larger quantities than ever before.

Miserable as depressing is, I would be remiss if I did not point out that it is useful if we do not use it for too long. For example, when someone close to you dies, a few months of depressing, which we call mourning, is extremely helpful to regain control over your life. Mourning helps keep inappropriate anger in check and helps you to gain support from your family and friends. Far from resenting your attempts to control them, those close to you welcome a chance to show they care. Only if the mourning begins to interfere with current relationships does it become ineffective and self-destructive.

In any severely frustrating situation, a short period of passive, inactive depressing—several hours to several weeks—helps us to avoid hasty, angry behaviors that might make an out-of-control situation considerably worse. Depressing may be painful, but it is safe. If more people depressed when they lost control, there would be much less violence in our society. Regardless of the situation, however, there are many times when the best behavior is to do as little as possible, and depressing is often that behavior.

Later, when we look at psychosomatic illness, I will explain that these self-destructive diseases often occur in people who do not use painful feeling behaviors to attempt to take charge of their lives. Miserable as they are, these behaviors often give us enough control to prevent our bodies from getting involved in the disease process. Even suicide is less likely in a person who is strongly depressing than in someone who has tried depressing and found it does not give the control he or she is looking for. If you have a friend or family member whose life continues to be seriously out of control, who has been depressing for months, and then stops for no apparent reason, you should be cautioned that he or she may now be considering suicide. In this instance, when that person stops depressing, it is because things are getting worse, not better.

As we go through life encountering a variety of frustrations, we diversify and learn additional feeling behaviors to supplement the angering with which we are born and the depressing that we soon learn. Each of us becomes adept in the use of a small group of these powerfully controlling behaviors, usually specializing in a few and sometimes in only one if it works well.

These additional behaviors—such as anxietying, guilting, and headaching—are very different from each other, and why anyone chooses one rather than the other depends on what that person may have created or learned and his or her evaluation of how effective any one behavior is. Most people find that one works better for them than others. Carol is a world-class depresser, and Phyllis an expert guilter. But when Carol gets too controlling with her depressing, Phyllis has also learned to migraine as a way of escaping Carol's control. Regardless of what the behaviors are, however, they are all chosen for those same reasons.

To gain more understanding of how people use these painful behaviors, let us take a look at a few people you may recognize. Randy was a highly intelligent college student who, as an undergraduate, made almost straight A's. He continued his success through the first year of the graduate school in business, but in his final year, he became suddenly incapacitated with fearing and anxietying. He chose to be anxious so strongly that he could not sit through an entire class. If he forced himself to stay, he increased his anxietying to the point where he felt a total panic, as if he were doomed to die immediately unless he left the room. His stomach became queasy, his hands sweated, his heart pounded, his ears buzzed, and his mouth became so dry that he could not speak coherently. Although he was easily able to do A work on all assignments, he could not pass the course unless he took the final exam in class, so he was stymied. In his quality world he had the picture of becoming a highly successful business executive. In the real world he was suddenly an unsuccessful graduate student. The last thing he thought was that he was choosing what he was doing.

Randy saw himself as excessively shy and unattractive and believed that no matter how well he did in school, no one would hire him. If he succeeded in school, he would have to face the real world and possibly find out that he could never be the successful executive in his quality world. But he enjoyed his academic success too much to drop out of school, so he took control by fearing to go to class and anxietying if he went. Through these behaviors, he gained painful control over his anger at not being attractive and gregarious. He was also able to ask for help with the school problems his behavior was causing. When he learned through counseling to take charge of his life, he finished school with honors. Maintaining this control and continuing to work very hard, in a few years he became vice president of a very successful company.

Mary is another example. Mary attempted to control her husband through her overwhelming fear of leaving the house. Psychologists call this incapacity a phobia. There are tens of thousands of people like her and many more with a variety of other phobias ranging from fear of flying to fear of germs. She would leave the house only in the company of George, her husband, or Janet, her daughter. She convinced herself, her family, her minister, and her physician that she had no responsibility for her disability. She was suffering from agoraphobia (fear of the marketplace), a disease of the nervous system. How she caught this disease was unclear, but there was a clue in her recollection that her mother suffered from a similar condition.

On the rare occasions when Mary had to leave the house (when it was being fumigated, for example), she suffered from the same anxietying symptoms that Randy did, so she stayed home and kept her husband a virtual prisoner except when he was at work. Even when he called her, as he frequently did to reassure her, she sometimes let the phone ring a while before she answered—a powerfully controlling ploy. She told him she was afraid to pick up, as someone might overhear and learn that she was alone. Every once in a while, he had to leave work to come home because she didn't answer the phone when he called.

In her internal world, Mary had the picture of a wonderful marriage with a strong, devoted husband. In the real world, she had not had a good marriage. She saw her husband as a weak man who was successful in business only because she pushed him to work hard. With success, he became resistant to her pushing, so more and more she satisfied her need for power by controlling him through her choice of phobicking. She kept him at her beck and call all day with calls to his office for things he had to do for her because she was afraid to leave the house. Mary also wanted to control her daughter, but Janet escaped to college and came home as little as possible.

Mary's fear of leaving the house controlled her anger, satisfied her need for power, and got her a great deal of attention as a sick person. It is interesting that after years of being prisoner, George left her without warning and made a new life for himself. Her control was too much. Her daughter had the strength not to get drawn in to replace her father, so Mary, no longer able to control anyone with her phobicking, and short of money, pulled herself together. She got a job, made friends, and has a better life than she has had for years.

We will usually give up behaviors that don't work if we are capable of better ones. Mary was. People who don't understand choice theory look at this as a miracle cure, but Mary has an idea that no miracles were involved.

Our next example, Richard, never liked his job as an insurance adjuster, but it paid adequately, and he felt trapped into it by financial responsibility. One day he lifted a heavy bottle for the office water cooler and says he heard his back snap as it gave out. He did suffer a mild back injury that probably healed in weeks, but he was immediately incapacitated and remains that way four years later. He has survived two back surgeries and over $150,000 worth of medical care. His back hurts worse than ever, he spends almost all his time in bed, and it is doubtful that he will ever return to work.

To test whether his pain was physical or mental, a doctor gave him an anesthetic drug that produces a mild hypnotic trance but does not kill pain. Under its influence, Richard was able to follow the suggestion that he get up from bed, bend, hop, and lift with no pain—activities he would not have been able to perform if his backache had a physical cause. He needed full consciousness to concentrate on this painful choice, and the drug broke his concentration to the point where he could no longer backache. When he was shown movies of himself doing all the exercises during the test, in a vain effort to prove to him that he is not disabled, he continued to be in control by saying, "That is what I have been telling you for years. I'd be fine if you would give me some real medicine. Can't I have more of that wonderful drug?" Of course, he can't live in a trance, so while the experiment was good "medicine" to protect him from further surgery, it did nothing to help him take charge of his life. No medicines that chemically affect the brain can be, in themselves, rehabilitative.

It is easy to see how backaching gets the anger at being in a hated job under good, if painful, control. Many people who see doctors in their offices and many of our hospital patients are like Richard, professional patients who learn to use paining as their way of dealing with life situations that are intolerable to them. Some people call this chosen pain imaginary, but it is not; this pain, like all pain, is real. If Richard's pain could be measured, it would be more intense than if he had something physically wrong with his back. When we are injured, we have as much pain as we need to do something about it.

This usually requires much more pain than the limited and localized pain necessary to immobilize an injured body part.

It is very important that the reader not conclude that I am claiming that all aches and pains—whether in the head, joints, back, neck, abdomen, or anywhere else—are chosen by the person who suffers from them. If there is a good medical reason—for example an injury, a new disease process, or some congenital defect—then medical diagnosis and care plus rest is always the best treatment. The diagnosis of paining should be considered only when there is no definite cause and when rest or good medical treatment is ineffective.

Richard was probably healed in about six weeks; after that time he was paining for the reasons cited earlier. Almost any chronic ache in the back, neck, or joints starts as an injury, but in many cases it continues as paining after the injury heals. Of course, an injured body part, even after it heals, may be weakened or adversely affected by scar tissue and prone to reinjury. In the case of a back injury, the person has to be careful about heavy lifting and violent twisting exercise like playing basketball or aerobic dancing.

I realize that it is very hard to accept that your pain may not be physical, especially if this is not confirmed by your physician. You must be aware that most physicians are too cautious to suggest a psychological cause to patients in severe pain even when they can find no physical cause. They don't believe that because they can't find it, it does not exist. But with all the exhaustive tests and X-ray capacity now available, it is extremely uncommon for the physical cause of a severe pain to elude a competent physician. If your doctor tells you she can find no cause and the pain has persisted for more than three months, you may want to reflect on the amount of satisfaction you have in your life. Facing that you may be paining is a big step in the direction of taking charge of your life.

Suppose you do conclude that you are paining and set about regaining control of your life, and later it turns out that the pain had a physical cause that was treatable. You have still done yourself no harm and probably a lot of good, because the more you are in charge of your life, the more effective any treatment will be. I do not suggest that you draw this conclusion without seeking good medical care and resting any injury for several months. If, however, the doctor can find no physical cause and the pain does not steadily decrease with rest but gets worse, and if it tends to subside when you are happy and recur when you are frustrated, you should suspect you are choosing to pain and treat yourself by attempting to regain control of your out-of-control life.

Our final example, Terri, washes her hands fifty times a day compulsively and calls her obsession with cleanliness crazy. She has been married to John almost twenty years and has little excitement or sexual satisfaction in her marriage. She is attractive, and men are attentive to her. She claims that the only thing wrong with her life is her compulsion, and although she makes fun of John, she does not relate her hand washing to him. In her quality world, however, is a picture of a far different marriage from the one she has.

Some time before she became, to use her own words, crazy clean, she got an offer from Fred, an attractive married man they see socially. In a gentle, joking way, she turned him down but not off, and she continues to enjoy the genteel attention she gets from this mild flirtation. John laughed when she told him about Fred and said maybe she shouldn't be so virtuous. This surprised her, but rather than pursue what, if anything, he meant, she simply didn't mention it anymore. But she upped her soap-and-water time significantly and is now busy day and night with cleanliness and personal hygiene.

Terri is safe. As long as she carries on so compulsively, she has no time to stray. How long she will be able to keep her life under clean control, I don't know, but if she doesn't do something to get more fun and excitement, she will literally scrub herself away. She shares her craziness with millions of other women who find themselves locked into a lifetime of no fun, no excitement, and little sex. Some wash as she does; many more depress, phobic, headache, backache, stomachache, and anxiety. They also eat to excess, drink, and use addicting drugs, legal and illegal. Many husbands do the same. Any time we lock ourselves into an unhappy relationship, we will struggle in painful and self-destructive ways to get out or improve the relationship. Many of these ways we choose—as Terri is choosing to wash, and Susan is choosing to depress—but there are many more we do not choose.

Some of those are irrational mental behaviors like psychoses, and others are irrational physiological behaviors best called psychosomatic disease, but based on my clinical experience, I believe either can become part of a self-destructive effort to regain control over our lives. When we are unable to satisfy our needs over a long period of time, we are like a starving person who will eat anything. I once read about a man marooned at sea who eventually ate toothpaste and leather shoe soles to alleviate his hunger. In the same way, while none of us wants to be crazy or sick, these actions can become a part of a desperate effort to regain control of our lives. I will explain how we make these forced, irrational choices in later chapters when I discuss creativity and reorganization. I mention them here to make it clear that I do not claim that we choose all of our misery. We do, however, choose the painful behaviors discussed in this chapter, and I think I am safe in saying that we choose most of the misery that we suffer.

6. Creativity and Reorganization

Every once in a while a story appears in my local newspaper about a successful middle-aged man who has abandoned his career; and after three years of scrimping, saving, and backbreaking work, has almost finished building a huge sailboat in his backyard and has a plan to sail the South Seas. As he shows the newspaper reporter through his beautiful creation, he seems ecstatically happy. His story is that having been unsatisfied and mildly depressed for years, he suddenly got the sailing bug. He admits he has never been to sea; in fact, he has never been past the breakers of the beach at Venice, California, so when asked where his creative idea came from, he smiles and says he really doesn't know. It just appeared one day, refused to go away, and here he is, almost ready to sail.

As I read this human-interest story, I am happy for him as well as a little envious. I secretly wish I could do something similar to break the routine of my life before I get too old. I quickly dismiss the thought for practical reasons, but even as I put the thought out of my mind, I wish I were as creative as some people seem to be. Then I too could make a big move in a new direction. It is my observation that most of us tend to have a low opinion of our creativity. We think of it as a special gift that a few lucky people possess but we'll never have. This is unfortunate, because we are all much more creative than most of us realize.

Unlike machines, all living organisms are not only highly creative but are always in the process of creating new behaviors. As I described in an earlier chapter, we never run out of things to do, think, or feel. Whether we are in control of our lives or not, new behaviors are constantly being made available to us through a remarkable creative process that I would like to call *reorganization*. All the things we already know how to do, think and feel—that is, all the actions currently available to us as part of our existing behavioral systems—can best be described as *organized behaviors*. We use them day after day to maintain control of our lives. Even miserable feeling behaviors, such as depressing, are part of this well-organized repertoire from which we always try to select the best possible behavior to satisfy a current picture. Some of these behaviors we created and many we learned from others around us, but either way they are no longer new.

The behavioral system is a two-part system. One part contains our familiar organized behaviors; the other part, which is the source of our creativity, contains the building blocks of all behaviors in a constant state of reorganization. By themselves, these building blocks could not be recognized as discrete actions, thoughts, or feelings; but I visualize this source of creativity as a kind of churning pot of disorganized behavioral material, a maelstrom of jumbled feelings, thoughts, and potential actions that are in a constant state of reorganization.

As active as this process is, we may have little or no awareness that it is going on. The one time we almost always become aware of reorganization is when we dream. Our dreams seem to be creative attempts to deal with the frustrations of the previous day, and crazy as they may be, they seem to help us control our lives by resting our minds. If we take sleeping pills, we tend to paralyze our ability to dream normally, and we do not get the restful sleep we need to maintain our health.

From this bubbling, ongoing creative reorganization comes a random stream of mostly minimal but occasionally well-organized new behaviors that are available to us to try if (1) we pay attention to them and (2) we decide that they may help us gain or regain control over our lives. It was from this creative system that the boat builder got the kernel of the new idea that led him to a life totally foreign to the well-organized existence he had led for years.

But if new behaviors are always available, why, for example, do we continue to depress or headache for as long as most of us do? The answer is deceptively simple: we continue to choose misery because what our reorganization systems create and offer to us may be no more effective than what we have. All our creative system can do is create—come up with new behaviors. There is no guarantee that what it creates has value to us or anyone else. During a week of strong depressing, we may create many new behaviors but continue to depress because not one of them, in our judgment, is as effective as our present misery.

The new behaviors offered to us may be unacceptably violent (to strangle the man who fired us from our job) or unacceptably crazy (to go to bed and stay there forever), neither of which in our opinion is better than our present well-organized choice to depress. We may seem to create faster when we are out of control, but more likely it only seems that way because when we are out of control, we are much more on the lookout for something new than when we are in good control. But fast or slow, our reorganization systems may never come up with anything better than what we have.

Only living organisms can create new behaviors. The most complex computer imaginable can only produce countless variations on the organized functions stored in its memory. It may take a long time, but after it has exhausted its capacity to vary what it has, it will run dry. A computer is like a gifted editor who can do wonders with what others write but does not write new material on her own. Our brains—or more precisely, the behavioral systems of our brains—are like the writer: always in the process of creating new behaviors, but much of what our brains create may have little or no value. In a sense, the creative part of the behavioral system is the writer and the organized part the editor. No matter how creative his intentions, if the man with the dream of sailing to the South Seas did not have organized carpentry skills, he could not have built the boat.

Because we are constantly reorganizing, our chances of finding one or more creative behaviors that will help us to achieve control of any frustrating situation is greatly increased. Any time a behavior we create helps us to achieve increased control, that behavior is stored in the behavioral system as an organized behavior ready to use in any situation where it may work. Many of the newly created behaviors that we accept and put to work in our lives are minimal and become tiny new creative variations of old, well-organized behaviors. For example, a slightly more efficient way to do your job is a small but welcome bit of creativity. At times, however, especially when our lives are dominated by painful choices, we accept much larger and more significant new ways to behave.

Mary, mentioned in chapter 5, may lock herself in her house based on her well-organized choice to phobic because she has not yet found a more effective way to control her present life. If her fear of leaving the house does not give her enough satisfaction, as it usually will not, she will continue to examine the reorganized alternatives she is constantly creating. These may be gibberish, however—a series of crazy thoughts and feelings that have no bearing on the frustrations of her life. As she continues to immobilize herself at home, the idea of suicide may begin to flicker through her mind, perhaps starting with the minimal idea, "Face it, there is a way to rid yourself of your pain."

The way the creative system works is that new ideas do not usually appear in their final form. An idea may start as a tiny thought, a different feeling, or some combination of both. If we entertain it, it tends to grow in an irregular, unpredictable fashion until we slowly become aware that we might put it into action. In Mary's case, if the pain of her choice to phobic becomes extreme and staying home becomes lonelier as her family and friends avoid her, the idea of putting the creative suicide notion into action becomes more attractive.

Finally, she may attempt the creative act of suicide to try to regain control over the people she can no longer control with her phobicking. If her suicide attempt is serious, she may succeed in regaining control for a while and make repeated attempts as needed. Keep in mind that what we create and try through reorganization does not have to be new under the sun—only new to us. Suicide, a well-known behavior, is always new to the person who attempts it. The wheel has been invented many times, but to the small child who reinvents it when he rolls a heavy toy box across the floor on some marbles, it is an exciting discovery.

Driven by our ever-present needs, we require a large supply of behaviors to deal with ourselves and the world around us. Most of us have learned enough behaviors that we usually believe we can handle the big issues in our lives: we see ourselves as well organized. But even the most effective among us often become frustrated by countless small irritations, such as flat tires, rainy days, and missed phone calls—frustrations we encounter far more frequently than major setbacks like losing a good job or breaking a leg. These small, unrelenting frustrations of daily living cause us to make constant demands on our behavioral systems for new behaviors to help us remain well organized and effective.

Our behavioral systems often answer these demands; new ideas do pop out of our ongoing reorganization into our minds and are continually put to use in our daily lives. These ...

New behaviors are usually simple and individually almost inconsequential, but added together over a period of time, they shape and reshape the way we deal with the world: they become our personalities.

It is this constant reorganization creating a stream of new ways to do, think, and feel that makes each of us a unique human being. Our individuality tends to take on a pattern, but even this pattern continues to change as we constantly add creativity in small—and occasionally large—doses to the way we behave.

If you focus on it, you can easily become aware of how creative you are—for example, when you bake a cake. For you, baking is a well-organized behavior that you have used many times to produce good cakes and cookies. It is one of thousands of similar, well-organized behaviors well known to you because you use them frequently, but they change as you continue to upgrade them with creative additions. Say you are assembling the ingredients and find you have no sugar. As you attempt to cope with this hardly earth-shaking problem, your reorganization gives you the hint that there may be a substitute for sugar. Looking around, you see a can of apple-juice concentrate. You say, "Why not?" and try it. This reorganization is minor—it pales beside the insights of Leonardo da Vinci—but it is new to you, and you gain a satisfying sense of control when the cake tastes good.

For years people have surfed and sailed, both enjoyable ways to play on the water. Then several years ago, someone, probably while sailing or surfing, got the creative idea of combining the two sports. This new twist has become so popular that sailing surfboards are now seen on recreational waters all over the world. I doubt that the inventor sat down and figured it out; I suspect the idea just came. What took a lot of figuring was how to design a board and a sail that would function together, and this, I am sure, involved a lot of creativity. Think of a regular thing you do, and then look back, and I am sure you will see many creative improvements that you have added over the years. When I write, for example, what I now do on a computer is as different from what I did when I started as day from night. But long before I began to use the word processor, I had figured out many ways to organize my writing that made it more efficient with each book. It is impossible to keep doing anything the same way; we always reorganize and improve in a myriad of small, creative ways—and while we do, we probably reject as worthless an equal number of improvements.

Occasionally we read a story in the newspaper about someone who has survived a plane crash in an isolated and barren location with no food. None of the survivor's organized eating behaviors worked, but he reorganized and ate something that he had never thought was edible, like insects, and stayed alive. In this extreme example, it was create or die, and books have been written about people in extreme situations who have even eaten human flesh to stay alive.

Creative as your reorganization system is, however, it may not come up with a successful behavior by the time you need it. All it can do is generate new behaviors, and even though you may be desperate, what it offers may have no relationship to what you need. It might offer you ideas like standing on your head and meditating as a way to fill your stomach or playing the kazoo as a way to make a living. But if you are severely frustrated, as your frustration grows, you become more and more susceptible to wild and even dangerous offers because you have nowhere else to turn to get anything better. Effective or ineffective, when you run out of all you know, reorganization in the hope of finding something new is all you have.

Most of us will never find ourselves in situations where we must create or die, and we deal reasonably well with most of our frequent frustrations through established, well-organized behaviors readily available in our behavioral systems. It is not often that we are even aware of any pressing need for the creativity that our random reorganization systems continually provide. It would seem logical that when there is no demand for creativity, the reorganization system would shut down, but it never does. This is probably because, from an ancient survival standpoint, the ability to create is by far the most important function of our behavioral systems. No species that shuts down its creative system could compete successfully against those who never stopped creating.

Therefore, even without any frustration or particular need for anything new at the time, each creative system idles along. It constantly sticks its nose into our business, gently popping new ideas into awareness. Most of these are rejected with little or no consideration, but frequently, with little awareness of what we are doing, we accept small creative improvements in organized behavior.

Since I have become aware of this creative system's existence, I can't say that I am measurably more creative, but I am more aware of what it offers and more open to its suggestions than I was before I knew about it. I believe that if we know of its existence, we will tend to listen more to its usually quiet suggestions and give more of them the careful consideration they may deserve.

As brothers and sisters or even twins grow and reorganize uniquely, they may become so different that they hardly seem to come from the same family. One reason that some rise from humble beginnings and others never do is probably successful reorganization. Sometimes this is just good luck, but more often it's the willingness to take a chance and tap the creativity that is inside all of us. As we begin the process of sexual development, we begin the search for satisfying sexual behaviors; and we do considerable reorganizing. Most of us add some creative aspects to our basic heterosexuality, but a significant number of people reorganize and find that homosexuality and other less usual sexual practices satisfy them. As I discussed in chapter 3, once we get a distinct picture of a sexually satisfying activity, we tend to keep that picture in our quality worlds even though it may not be socially acceptable. Why we do this so rigidly is yet unclear.

When we are very young, we reorganize continually, because it is the only way we can learn the countless behaviors we need to fulfill our needs. Moments after birth, we start adding creative additions to our total behaviors that seem sensible to us. These are the beginnings of our personalities, and even day-old infants have recognizable personalities to the trained eye and differ from each other markedly. Infants are similar for only a few moments after birth, and then they start the lifelong process of changing into who they will become.

Creativity is the invention of something new that has never before existed in the life of its creator. There will always be those rare occasions when something new and highly beneficial to everyone is created, as when the first human—perhaps a woman—who had the anatomy for speech fortuitously reorganized and spoke. Speech gave her and those she spoke to—who then learned to speak—such an evolutionary advantage that we are all descended from her and them. There is probably no human who does not have some remnant of her genes, but to speak as early as we do, each one of us still reorganizes much as the first person did. For each of us, it is not only imitation but also a creative act to do so. If you waste your time foolishly trying to teach a little baby to speak, you will have no success and may even interfere with the normal process of reorganization that he or she is using to learn this complex behavior.

Creativity very often will provide the individual with more control over his or her life. But if it does not, it is not the fault of the creative process. If there is a fault, it is with how we, aware of it or not, decide to use this process. In and of itself, the reorganization system does not know right from wrong, good from bad, artistic from crass, scientific from silly. It doesn't even know dumb from smart. All it knows is to create and to keep creating. If we use what it creates to take more effective charge of our lives, this is fortuitous, but it is not and never will be the purpose of reorganization. Its only purpose is to create. If it had any other purpose, it would not work.

If a behavior that your reorganization system creates leads you to choose a self-destructive act—such as suicide—there is no sense blaming this on the system, because, having no purpose except to create, it cares nothing about keeping us alive. If it were designed to keep us safe, it would be unable to offer us any behavior that might be dangerous. But dangerous, unorthodox behaviors have been at the forefront of much that has proved valuable. Therefore, we cannot be truly creative if our creativity is in any way biased. As soon as any creative system has bias, it must lose creativity in the area of the bias. Reorganization is always random and unpredictable. If it were not, it could not be truly creative. Columbus never would have sailed if his reorganization system had been biased toward believing the earth was flat. And if someone comes to you and convinces you to invest a thousand dollars in a process to make electricity from moonbeams, it could turn out to be the best investment you ever made.

Creativity is only as valuable as any of us decides it is, and progress depends on how much we can convince others that our decision is correct. This tends to be a slow process; people do not easily or quickly give up their old, well-organized behaviors for new ones. It took the Catholic Church over four hundred years to make up its collective mind that Galileo was creative, not heretical, so don't be impatient and stop listening to your creativity if what you discover is not immediately proclaimed as progress.

7. Craziness, Creativity, and Responsibility

Many years ago, a mother of a young man told me her son had broken down while attending college, and she made an appointment for him to see me. She said he was both willing and able to come and see me on his own, and she was right. When he came, he shook my hand, sat down, and, as far as I could tell, looked fine. I asked him to tell me a little about himself, and he said nothing. I tried again and suddenly realized that, in his own creative way, he had decided to say nothing. When I asked if he would talk to me and explained that talking was the way I worked, he indicated by shaking his head that he would not. He would answer yes or no by a shake of his head. That was all. His behavior was mildly but definitely crazy. He had reorganized and accepted the creative idea that if he gave up speaking he would, in some way that made sense to him, regain control over his life. After he put this newly created idea into practice, it became an organized, need-fulfilling behavior that he chose to use with everyone.

Not speaking had a powerful controlling effect on his parents and the family doctor, and I am sure he expected both to frustrate and to intimidate me with this symptom. I did not know choice theory then, but I recognized that his refusal to talk was crazy and that if he could control me with this symptom, I could not help him.

I told him that it did not make any difference to me whether he talked now or later; I would wait. I added that as long as he refused to talk, I would talk to him. I told him that I didn't usually have such a captive listener, and I was encouraged that he smiled. Then, more seriously, I explained that it would probably be deadly boring to listen to me for an entire hour, but if all he would do was nod yes or shake no, I would have to do my best with this limited exchange.

At this, he grimaced. I said that I would make no demands upon him to talk outside my office. In choice theory terms, all he would lose was control over me for an hour; all the others whom he controlled by his muteness he could continue to control. He agreed, started to talk, and told me his story, and in a few months we worked out a better way for him to take control of his life. He is now a television producer with a family and no more creativity than is normal for his profession.

When he first came to see me, he thought he would not be responsible for anything he did as long as he was crazy. He was prepared to control me with his craziness just as he had controlled quite a few people before he met me. Had he succeeded, as do many people who reorganize with crazy behaviors, he might have taken a great deal longer to get his life organized than the six months I worked with him. There is hardly a more effective controlling behavior than craziness, because almost no one, including some mental-health and legal professionals, understands that although the initial idea is a creative reorganization, the decision to put the idea into practice is not. Any reorganization that is put into use becomes an organized behavior. If it does not work to help the user gain control, it may be given up; but as long as it is used, even though it may be crazy, it is organized for the user.

In frustrating situations, when you begin to run out of organized behaviors to satisfy your needs, you will necessarily begin to pay more attention to what your creative system offers. The more you lose control, the more you will consider trying an idea like not talking, and if it works, you will start to use it. (In this case, not talking removed this young man from what was for him a very frustrating situation.) All of us are potentially capable of creating new behaviors, and if we start to use them, these behaviors may be judged crazy by those around us. But if my life is out of control and craziness gets it more in control, then for me craziness becomes an organized behavior. It worked so well for the young man in my example that he went along with it for a while.

Crazy creativity is anything you do that most of us who are sane judge to be very different from what we would do in a similar situation. The whole gamut of what are called mental illnesses, including hallucinations and delusions, are creative behaviors. If I know what a voice is, I am perfectly capable of creating a new voice in my mind that I actually hear. All of us do this when we dream, but because we all do it and few of us act on our dreams, we don't call it crazy. While there are no restrictions on what we create, we are more likely to put tangible creations to work in our lives than gibberish. Other people tend to pay more attention to what they recognize, and they don't recognize gibberish, so we get more control over those around us by saying we hear voices. If you are desperate, even a behavior you recognize as crazy is acceptable to you if it gives you some control.

To take effective charge of our lives, we must learn that although we are not responsible for what we create, crazy or sane, we are responsible for what we choose to do with our creations. If I had dealt with this young man as mentally ill, the victim of some physical or chemical brain derangement that had happened to him and for which he had no responsibility, he might still be in treatment—still controlling me and others with his muteness. My responsibility was not to let him control me and at the same time to teach him more effective ways to take charge of his life. Abnormal as what we create may be, our creativity itself is a normal, ongoing process, and when we put it into practice, it is not illness. If we call it mental illness and excuse the creator from any responsibility for what he or she does, we do the creator and our society a disservice.

There was public outcry when John Hinckley Jr. was found not guilty for his 1981 shooting of President Reagan and others because of mental illness. According to accepted psychiatric thinking as interpreted by federal courts, the shooting was a product of mental illness over which he had no control. This seemed wrong to the general public—and from a choice theory standpoint, the public was right and the courts were wrong.

Hinckley was a young man with many frustrations. Lonely and powerless, he struggled unsuccessfully for years to fulfill his needs. Like all of us, he reorganized constantly; but unlike most of us, he acted on his innate creativity more readily than we do, because he had so few organized behaviors that worked for him. But he still had control over the part of his creativity that he chose to put into practice, and in his case it is obvious that what he chose to do was to control someone else. Crazy as it was, he decided that he would have more control over his life if he shot the president than if he behaved in a different way, and he is responsible for that decision. He is not responsible for getting the idea—we all get crazy ideas—but he is responsible for putting it into practice.

When any crazy, creative act affects someone else, we have to assume that control is the purpose whether or not the other person is known to the perpetrator of the act. Only when a behavior is totally without observable external purpose—that is, purely creative and without observable effect on anyone or anything except the perpetrator—can that behavior be judged as something for which the perpetrator is not responsible. A man who sits at home staring at the wall, totally unwilling to eat or talk, is not responsible at this time, because he is still immersed in the act of reorganizing. This behavior is passive. If there is activity, then there is purpose to the behavior, and it is no longer pure reorganization. If a person gets in a car or takes out a gun and runs amok, spreading death and destruction to total strangers, these are organized behaviors that cannot be performed in a state of total reorganization, and it would be wise to handle them as criminal acts. To carry out these acts requires a much greater awareness of external purpose than is exhibited by the man who is in a chair totally involved in his own creativity.

If, after committing a crime, the criminal reverts to total reorganization, he should not be tried until he is enough in charge of his life to stand trial. If he never gains that control—a situation that almost never happens—then he should be treated in a hospital as long as he lives. Any creative act that is not a crime should be treated as a psychological problem if the person wants to be treated. If he or she does not want treatment, the case should be resolved according to whatever law applies, but my belief is that someone who does not infringe on the rights of others should not be forced to take drugs or receive treatment for putting his or her creativity into practice. This does not mean that we should not try to convince people they need treatment; this is done all the time and is an integral part of any good mental health program.

If a young woman—who is by our standards slender enough to be attractive—reorganizes and puts the crazy thought into action that she can satisfy her needs better by being much thinner than she is, we call her anorexic. We often go further and say that she is suffering from a disease called anorexia nervosa and therefore is not responsible for her choice not to eat. Her creativity may lead her to the well-organized behavior of starving herself, and although this is patently crazy, if she dies, who is responsible? It makes little sense to say that her disease was responsible and that we could not treat it.

What is sensible is to understand that she has embarked on a crazy course, keeping in mind that she is responsible for choosing this course. She is starving herself not because she wants to die but because she has decided that becoming thinner and still thinner is the best way to take charge of her life. As she continues to lose weight, she makes the discovery that her refusal to eat gets her unbelievable power over her mother, father, many of the doctors who treat her, and others. Corrupted by this absolute power, she continues to refuse to eat. When she talks about how attractive she is now, what she is really talking about is how much power she has to control everyone around her.

Our job is to try to help her satisfy her needs in a less crazy way and to keep her alive while we try to give her the help she needs to find a better behavior than starvation. But she is just as responsible for choosing to starve as Einstein was for giving us insight into the secrets of the universe. Creativity is creativity. It is no less creative because it is crazy or self-destructive, and we are no less responsible because, lacking something better, we act on what we create.

The vast majority of those who act on their creativity are not criminal; they are like this young woman. Too often, however, if their creativity is far from what we accept as normal, we lock them up in a mental hospital and give them powerful drugs that paralyze not only their creativity but their whole behavioral systems. Even organized behaviors like walking and talking are made difficult by these drugs; feelings are almost totally eliminated, and thinking is greatly impaired. Since they can regain control only through organized behaviors, in my opinion, paralyzing the whole system to knock out crazy creativity is excessive treatment. What they need is not drugs but effective counseling to help them become better organized. They need to be locked up in a mental hospital only if they are a danger to themselves or others.

We can and should learn to recognize that when we lose control, we may begin to become aware of our ongoing reorganization, and we should not be afraid of this normal process. A young woman once told me that when the frustrations of her taxing job occasionally piled up beyond her control, she noticed what she described as her personality slipping away. She thought she was losing her mind, because she was becoming aware of a series of thoughts and feelings that seemed to her totally inappropriate to the situation with which she was struggling at the time. Rapid random thoughts flooded her mind almost as if she were in a bad dream, and she began to choose to panic in an effort to deal with the strange and frightening things going on in her head. She had an overwhelming urge to leave work, run home, crawl into bed, and try to deny the existence of her jumbled mind. She asked me if she was going crazy.

I told her that she was not going crazy in the sense that she was on the road to permanent insanity. However, during these episodes, which lasted several minutes but seemed longer, she was crazy in the sense that she had no control over what she thought and felt. They occurred mostly in the middle of tense business meetings in which she had a lot of responsibility and absorbed a great deal of what she believed was unfair criticism. I explained to her that what she was describing was the initial awareness of her creative system that occurs when her organized behaviors are temporarily failing her. What was causing her to choose to panic was her realization that she was beginning to consider acting on some of this creativity, actions that would have been disastrous to her career. But I also pointed out the likelihood that she also got some very helpful creative ideas at these times, ideas that were part of the same random process. She laughed and agreed and was very receptive to my choice theory explanation of what was going on.

She has now incorporated a good working knowledge of choice theory into her life, so when she occasionally reorganizes, she realizes what is going on and has simple, well-organized behaviors ready to use when this occurs. She excuses herself for a moment, leaves the room to have a cup of coffee, or goes to the rest room. During this brief respite, she tells herself she has become aware of her ongoing reorganization because she is in a temporarily out-of-control situation. But she also tells herself that she knows she has the ability to reject her own creativity if it is not useful and to keep an open mind if it is. She is no longer worried about going crazy because she realizes that what she is experiencing is her normal creativity. She also knows that while this process is occurring, she need not choose to act upon it.

We can neither turn off our creativity nor avoid becoming aware of it when our lives are out of control. We can, however, learn that we do not have to accept what our creative systems offer if we can find an organized behavior to use for a while that will help us regain control. The young businesswoman decided to leave the meetings for a minute to take a walk, call a friend, bake a cake, or count to ten. Even a few minutes of a familiar, well-organized behavior will usually make us less aware of our ongoing reorganization. The more we know choice theory, the more we are likely to smile rather than panic during the infrequent occasions when we become aware that a lot of crazy creativity has entered into our thinking and feeling. With this knowledge, we are able to look past the craziness for ideas that are not crazy. We know they may be there, and if we wait and keep our minds open to them as they pop into awareness, our creativity can become more available to us than if we knew nothing about what was happening.

8. Psychosomatic Illness as a Creative Process

Few of us ever think of disease as a creative process. Yet just as insanity is an example of mental creativity, it is likely that most chronic illnesses are examples of physiological creativity. It is my contention that any chronic illness for which there is no known physical cause and no specific medical treatment may be our bodies' creative but inadvertent involvement in the struggle to satisfy our needs. In this group are some of our most common and disabling diseases, such as coronary artery disease, rheumatoid arthritis, eczema, ileitis and colitis. Unlike usually treatable diseases of known physical cause, such as tuberculosis and diabetes, or preventable diseases, such as polio, these are most likely the unwanted accompaniments of chronically out-of-control life situations. Often related to unhappy marriages or unsatisfying work, they are most aptly called psychosomatic.

Since there is no specific medical treatment for them, the best advice to give anyone suffering from a psychosomatic illness is that she should try to regain effective control over whatever in her life is out of control, perhaps an unwanted person in the house. Unfortunately, as even your doctor may recognize, this approach is not supported by our present medical delivery system, which tends to follow a scientific and mechanistic approach that treats the physical side of all diseases much more rigorously than the mental side. This impersonal medical approach makes it harder, not easier, for sick people to regain the control over their lives that I believe they need if they are to recover from these serious illnesses.

While I recognize that what I will explain in this chapter is controversial, I will make every effort to support what I claim with a clear choice theory exposition of how these diseases come into being. To avoid any possible misunderstanding, let me begin by explaining what is a disease and what is not.

For disease to exist, there must either be some structural change from normal to abnormal that can be seen either with the naked eye or under the microscope, or some life-endangering chemical or electrical malfunction, such as abnormal electrical impulse to the heart. Therefore, even though we may seek medical care for painful feeling behaviors like headaching or backaching, these are not diseases when there is no structural change in any tissue or organ and no dangerous chemical or electrical malfunction.

There may be temporary changes in structures, as in migraining, when there is a marked narrowing of some of the major blood vessels that supply the brain before and during the headache. The painful symptoms are thought to be related to these changes, but when the headache is over, the vessels return to normal, and when the migrainer gains effective control of his or her life, the headaches and the vascular changes disappear forever. Large changes in tension in the muscles of the back often are associated with a backache, but they too return to normal when the backache is over. I also want to make clear that a headache can be caused by an infection like meningitis, and a backache can be the result of a muscle spasm or slipped disk, so when I talk of migraining or backaching, I am referring to headaches and backaches for which rigorous medical examination has revealed no tissue damage.

Any disease, psychosomatic or not, always involves some observable structural abnormality in the part of the body involved in the disease or some dangerous conduction malfunction. In heart disease, there is narrowing of the coronary arteries, the vessels that supply the heart muscles with blood. In rheumatoid arthritis, there is swelling and inflammation of the involved joints. In eczema, there is reddening, oozing, bleeding, and loss of skin integrity; and in colitis, there is thickening, loss of elasticity, ulcerations, and loss of mobility in all or part of the large bowel. Disease may also involve temporary changes in nondiseased parts of the body. For example, along with heart disease there may be swelling of the legs as fluid accumulates. If the patient is treated properly, the fluid reabsorbs, and the legs return to normal. The heart, however, never returns to its prediseased state.

The known causes of noncreative diseases may be an external agent like a streptococcus or an internal malfunction like diabetes; but external or internal, what we see as the illness is how our bodies attempt to cope with these tangible causes. Creative diseases, such as rheumatoid arthritis, have no tangible cause; their origin is in a normal body function that, for no apparent physical reason, begins to function abnormally. In a creative disease like rheumatoid arthritis, our immune systems—whose normal function is to protect us from toxic external agents like streptococci or internal pathogens like cancer cells by attacking and neutralizing them before they can do serious harm—attack and may destroy a perfectly normal wrist joint as if it were foreign to our bodies.

These creative or psychosomatic diseases fill our hospitals today. Most of the threat of noncreative diseases like cholera, the plague, and smallpox, which at one time killed people by the millions, have long been brought under control by sanitation, pest control, and vaccination. In the past fifty years, medical science has also made tremendous progress in treating stubborn bacterial diseases like gonorrhea with antibiotics and viral diseases like polio through immunization. Even the latest feared disease, AIDS, is now known to be caused by the human immunodeficiency virus and may in time be brought under control by immunization.

Medical science has progressed enough so that if you contract a noncreative external disease you can be almost assured that it will be diagnosed correctly and treated successfully by your doctor. If it is a virus, there is a good chance that a successful immunization program is available or will be worked out in the near future if there are enough cases to warrant this effort. What medicine has yet to develop is a systematic method of dealing effectively with what I call the creative or psychosomatic diseases, because most medical education does not recognize that their cause may be our bodies' involvement in our attempt to regain effective control over some situation in our lives that is chronically out of control.

Alan, forty-four, has had a high-salary job for the past ten years. He works directly under JB, the owner of the company, who seems to delight in making Alan's job a living hell. He criticizes Alan for everything and gives him no credit for his obvious contribution to the company. Occasionally he even goes through the aggravating ceremony of firing him and then magnanimously calling him back and raising his pay. A day never passes when JB fails to remind Alan of his generosity. Alan is under JB's thumb but can't see his way clear to quit, as he has a family and a lifestyle that needs the support of JB's generous salary.

There is a huge difference between the ideal picture of work in Alan's quality world—where he is treated with respect and given some credit—and the way JB treats him. He is continually aware of urges to do something to reduce that difference, but short of quitting, he has not been able to figure out what. None of his organized behaviors work, and he is actively aware of some fairly crazy ideas as his creative juices boil as he looks for a way to take charge.

Much as he would like to throw in the sponge and depress, to keep his job he must keep a stiff upper lip to deal effectively with employees and customers all day long. Maintaining a cheerful facade is difficult, but he does it—as do many of us who are stuck in bad jobs or bad marriages or with children we cannot abide. But what Alan can't stop—nor does he want to, because of the pleasure they give him—are the creative thoughts that run through his mind day and night, mostly about a variety of satisfying ways to kill JB. The comforting fantasy that recurs over and over is the idea of slowly strangling him with his bare hands as JB gasps for mercy.

One day, after a particularly trying late-afternoon meeting during which he was fired once again, Alan goes home to find that his teenage son has put a deep scrape all along one side of Alan's classic Porsche while backing it out of the garage. The boy is heartbroken—he wanted to surprise Alan by polishing the car—and as Alan looks at the scrape in the sculptured lines, he is beside himself. That night he is awakened by a severe pain in his chest, is rushed to the hospital, and is diagnosed as having suffered a massive heart attack. He lingers between life and death in intensive care for two weeks but finally recovers enough to undergo bypass surgery to restore the impaired circulation to his heart.

He is sure his heart attack was caused by the stress of his job—the Porsche episode was the coup de grace—but, needing the income, he returns to work, where he begins to have chest pains almost immediately. His doctor advises him to consider retiring on the small disability that JB provides, but it would not be enough to begin to support his expensive lifestyle. Although he does not know choice theory, he knows that his life is seriously out of control and does not know how to take charge of it. In a later chapter, we will deal with how he might use knowledge of choice theory to do this, but now let us take a look at how his chronic frustration may have led his coronary arteries to occlude, a very common scenario.

All our physiology—the machinery of our bodies—is kept functioning and healthy under the well-organized direction of a small group of ancient brain structures generally referred to as the old brain. When you turn a page of this book, it is your old brain that provides your muscles with the power to move. Your heart rate and blood pressure are regulated by your old brain; if you feel your heart speed up while watching a scary or sexy movie, it is the old brain that actually causes this to happen. Your food is digested under its direction, and it regulates the hormones that greatly determine your sexual capacity. If you are lost in the desert, your old brain will send your new brain messages that you recognize as thirst and finally such painful, urgent thirst that it seems you have no choice but to search for water. It is only when your survival is threatened, however, or when you have had no sexual release for a long time, that the old brain attempts to direct the way you function through painful messages.

The old brain has nothing directly to do with any conscious behavior; it cares nothing about whether we satisfy needs like power or freedom, needs that Alan's new brain desperately cares about because they have been unsatisfied for so long. To satisfy these needs, the old brain takes direction from the large, newer, conscious part of the brain—the cerebral cortex or new brain. If, as often happens, the new brain asks the old brain to function beyond any of its well-organized or usual ways of functioning, it will begin to reorganize and may try some new and better way to function. In Alan's case, although he had no awareness that it was occurring, his new brain had long been making huge demands not only on his mind but also on his body, demands that led his old brain to the creative functioning that became his coronary artery disease. To understand how the new brain does this, let us take a detailed look at how it functions.

My new brain is the source of my consciousness: it contains my pictures, through which I must satisfy all of my needs, as well as my sensory camera with all its filters, and it directs all of my conscious behaviors. In essence, my new brain is me. But alone, my new brain can do nothing directly. All it can do is give orders that have to be carried out by my old brain, or I cannot function. By itself, it is a general without an army: it can give orders, but unless the old brain carries them out, nothing happens.

No one has to teach me to breathe, blink, digest my food, or maintain my blood pressure or heart rate. And although I have learned precisely how to move my muscles, as when I learned to walk or focus my eyes, no one had to teach me to move my muscles; I was born with this knowledge encoded in my old brain. What my new brain learns as it struggles to fulfill my needs is to give more and more specific and precise orders to do, think, and feel, which my old brain carries out with increasing accuracy until I grow quite old. Under the complete direction of my new brain, my old brain learns to provide the bodily wherewithal to carry out what my new brain asks of it. If I decide to think, it makes sure that the new brain has the blood and nutrients to perform this function. And if I feel ecstatic, it is because my old brain secretes some morphine-like chemicals that actually produce the ecstasy.

Most of the time, the old brain follows directions so quickly and efficiently that we pay no attention to what it is doing. But occasionally the new brain gives it an instruction that taxes its capacity to perform, as when you decide to run a marathon. The old brain has no trouble running; it is running twenty-six miles that gives it a problem. This is because it has its own built-in instructions to keep the body healthy, and the new brain is now asking it to pay no attention to these innate instructions. The old brain can't refuse to run the marathon, but it can send back to the new brain a series of messages to slow down or stop that are felt as pain and fatigue. The new brain, however, can disregard these messages, and the old brain can be finally so taxed that it fails to function normally, and if you still try to keep running, you may get sick, lose consciousness, or even drop dead.

Few of us run marathons, but most of us suffer an occasional disappointment when our old brain stubbornly refuses to follow instructions. For example, I decide to engage in sexual behavior to satisfy a new-brain need like love or power. This decision is strictly new brain—that is, I have sex frequently enough that there is no old-brain demand for sexual release. But to make love successfully depends on my old brain's willingness to get my sex organs ready. If I attempt to make love when I am physically exhausted, my old brain may decide for health reasons not to get my sex organs ready and I will not be able to make love. It is rare, however, that my old brain does not do as it is directed; these two examples are far more the exception than the rule.

If the old brain had the sense to refuse to follow instructions on more than these rare occasions, there would be much less psychosomatic disease. That it almost slavish attempts to carry out what it believes the new brain is commanding it to do is most likely what caused Alan's heart attack and what causes all other psychosomatic diseases. Several years ago a man died after collapsing from exhaustion during the Honolulu marathon. If you were the coroner in charge of investigating this death and you knew a little choice theory, you might begin by looking into the parts played by each of his brains. The evidence against his new brain is highly incriminating. It was this part of his brain, perhaps in a desperate effort to gain a sense of power through competitive running, which drove him to this fatal effort. As he ran, as all long-distance runners will testify, he received a barrage of electrical and chemical fatigue signals from his overtaxed old brain, all trying to tell his new brain to stop asking the old brain to push his body to this extreme.

All of us are conscious of these old-brain signals as fatigue, and their purpose is to persuade us to slow down and take a rest. When they come hard and heavy, as in a marathon, it is almost impossible to disregard them. If the runner's new brain had been more sensible, it would have given the order to stop or at least to slow down. But he didn't have that sense, because in the past he had counted on his old brain, despite its complaints, to carry him through, and it had not let him down. Still, you certainly would not be remiss if you blamed his new brain for his death no matter how many successful marathons it had persuaded the old brain to run in the past.

There is, however, considerable evidence that his old brain was at fault too. It was given the assignment of running the marathon. It had run marathons before, and it should have figured out how to do it again. After all, the new brain can't pay attention to the whining of a lazy old brain, and it had every right to expect performance when it gave an order that had been carried out well in the past. To drop dead was rank insubordination, because when the old brain failed and died, the new brain had to die with it. This, of course, is one of the dangers the new brain should keep in mind when it gives such extreme orders. The old brain is such a good soldier that it might be signing its own death warrant.

When the old brain was pushed beyond its ability to continue to run, at that moment it had used up all the organized running behaviors that had worked for it in the past. Just as the new brain, when it runs out of things to do, think, and feel, begins to accept some newly organized psychological behaviors, the old brain also begins to accept some newly reorganized physiological behaviors. But as with the new brain, there is never any guarantee that the new physiological behaviors the old brain creates will be any better than the well-organized behaviors it has used since birth. Also, like the new brain, if the old brain judges that what it creates is no better than what it has, it will keep using what it has, inadequate though it may be, as long as it can. But finally, if what it has won't work at all—as in the case of the totally exhausted runner—it must take a chance and use a new physiological behavior in the hope that it can continue to keep running and stay alive.

Perhaps in the past the runner's old brain had reorganized and provided him with some new and stronger running behaviors. Maybe it figured out how to pump blood at a faster rate or metabolize waste products less poisonously, but this time none of those previously created effective behaviors were working. As it continued to reorganize, in desperation it came up with a new behavior that it tried in good faith but that proved fatal. The physiological behavior that caused his death was probably a newly created electrical signal that his old brain generated to stimulate his heart to pump more blood. This signal was so strong or so different from normal that it caused the ventricles of his heart to fibrillate. This newly created fatal arrhythmia caused the heart to beat so fast that it became totally inefficient and couldn't pump blood. Ventricular fibrillation, one of the two causes of sudden death (cerebral hemorrhage is the other), is always fatal in a few minutes unless it can be stopped. So, although the old brain let the new brain down, it was trying as creatively as it could to keep up with the new brain's excessive demands.

Was the death of the runner psychosomatic? I would say emphatically yes. It was the new brain (the psyche) that drove the old brain (the soma) to accept a fatal reorganization. Here we have a sudden, consciously motivated death, which is not usually considered psychosomatic, because most psychosomatic diseases are chronic, and we are not aware of the new brain's pushing the old. Yet there is no doubt that it fits all the criteria for such a disease perfectly, and Alan's heart attack was the same process in slow motion.

Alan had been fantasizing for years about strangling JB with no awareness that this new-brain thinking behavior was having a powerful effect on his old brain. Of course, the old brain knows nothing about strangling; in actuality it knows nothing at all about anything that the mind may desire. But it does know that if the mind gives the body an instruction, it has to get the body to carry it out as long as the instruction persists. When Alan's new brain pondered strangling, his old brain was immediately alerted—probably through receiving some new-brain electrical and chemical hormone messages—to get his body ready for a life-and-death physical struggle. The new brain sent this strong alert because it knew that tough old JB was not going to take being strangled without a fight.

But Alan had no intention of actually going through with the attack. He knew it was all fantasy. Still, the more he indulged it, the more get-ready-for-a-big-fight hormone messengers he poured into his old brain. The old brain does not know fantasy or reality; all it knows is to act on the hormones sent by the new brain and get the body ready for what it believes is an impending fight. It quickly takes care of business, and it keeps taking care of business as long as the get-ready hormones keep coming—in Alan's case he was ready to strangle for years. And then, on top of all this body preparedness, in his distress he sent a super-strong strangle-his-son message on the fatal day the Porsche was scraped.

Most physiologists believe that our bodies have not yet evolved to the point where we can handle chronic physiological tensions year after year and still stay healthy. Physically we are still too close to what we were only a few thousand years ago, when if we had the idea of strangling, we went ahead and started to strangle. We won or lost, but it was soon over, and we could relax. Chronic tension, produced by long-term fantasy messages from new brain to old, is a product of the complications of civilization. It can—and usually does—make us sick.

Perhaps the most common sickness associated with this kind of angering, the basic feeling behavior that kept Alan tensed up for strangling, is heart disease. As he remained chronically ready for a big fight, his old brain raised his blood pressure and increased his heart rate to ensure that his body would have enough blood for the fight. It also pumped clotting chemicals into his bloodstream so that if he was wounded he would not bleed to death. There is no harm if this goes on for a short time, but if it goes on for years and still no fight occurs, the cardiovascular system starts to wear out prematurely. It's like driving your car beyond the red line on the tachometer and wondering why the motor fails.

But even more happens. I believe that the old brain, in some automatic way, senses that this unrelenting state of physical tension— the body's constant readiness for a fight that never happens—is dangerous to good health. In order to maintain the integrity of the body, the old brain, acting desperately and automatically to preserve the body, alerts the immune system as if the chronic, never-ending tension were a foreign invader. As it searches for the invader, the immune system also reorganizes and becomes creative. This additional creativity often becomes destructive, as it did in Alan's case. It is a crazy kind of self-destructiveness; coronary artery disease, like most other psychosomatic diseases, is analogous to a psychosis of the body.

As the cardiovascular system is tensed for years on end, the blood rushing through the arteries begins to erode the artery walls and produce rough spots. The excess clotting elements already circulating are trapped by these rough spots and begin to form small clots at these sites. The immune system, seeing a clot that normally would not be there, somehow (no one yet knows why) becomes crazily creative and attacks the clot as if it were a foreign body. This quickly causes the clot to become inflamed, and the inflammation enlarges it, just as a scab on a skin wound is always larger than the initial blood clot. As time passes, the clot continues to enlarge through the repetition of this process until the clot obstructs the flow of blood through the artery. Alan suffered his heart attack when clots blocked one or more of the small but high-blood-flow arteries that fed his heart.

Two common causes of an acute heart attack involve diminished blood flow to the heart. First, as the heart receives less nourishment and becomes tired, there is a tendency for it to pump with decreased efficiency. As it does, it tries to compensate for this loss in efficiency by beating in more creative ways called arrhythmias. But if these creative arrhythmias produce less blood flow, as they often do, the sudden reduction of blood flow through the coronary arteries causes some measurable damage to the heart muscle, and often what is known as a heart attack. If the patient is alive when he or she reaches the hospital, modern treatment to stabilize the blood flow usually prevents an immediate fatality.

Another cause of a heart attack is a sudden clot completely blocking a coronary artery. Such an attack happens so quickly that the heart will often turn to reorganized electrical behavior and begin fibrillating, which is probably what happened to the marathon runner. Fibrillation is usually fatal in minutes unless it occurs in an ambulance or in a hospital, where it can sometimes be treated. Fortunately for Alan, he had the first kind of heart attack and has now had bypass surgery. This operation can have great value, partly because the blood supply is increased but also because the patient now believes that with this dramatic help he is in greater control of his life.

My belief is that the relationship between physical fitness and good overall health may be more indirect than direct; a good diet and aerobic exercise give those who practice them a much greater sense of control over their lives. If Alan continues to work for JB, he would be wise to follow such a program, because if he could grow to believe in it, he might be able not to take JB's antics seriously. If he learned some choice theory and began to understand how important it is for him to relax, and if he realized that physical fitness could provide the relaxation he needs, he might stop having the chest pains that may presage another heart attack.

There are many other psychosomatic diseases, and most, if not all, involve some reorganization of the immune system that drives it to attack normal tissue in an inadvertent effort to help the old brain carry out chronic, hard-to-satisfy instructions from a new brain that, like Alan's, has lost control. In the case of these diseases, the immune system's help is not only unneeded but disastrous. This attack on our own normal tissue by our immune system has caused medicine to label these diseases *autoimmune,* or self-induced. Although in different diseases it may attack different tissues or organs, the immune system always seems to reorganize in a crazy way that causes it to misread normal tissue as foreign tissue and then attack and destroy it as if it were foreign.

Why immune system creativity takes this form and why it attacks one tissue and not another are questions still unanswered. When this creative immunity attacks normal joints rheumatoid arthritis may be the diagnosis. When the spinal column is attacked, it may be called spondylitis; and when the gastrointestinal tract is attacked, the result may be ileitis or colitis. If it attacks the sheaths of the nerves, the diagnosis may be multiple sclerosis; the kidneys, glomerulonephritis; the skin, eczema. There are many other, more obscure autoimmune diseases, but these are among the most common. What I believe is common to almost all of them is a life like Alan's that is chronically out of control.

Since there are multiple, self-generated, random creative possibilities the brain may even become stronger and healthier as a result of reorganization. Certainly there are many examples of people who live long and healthy lives under what seem to be markedly adverse circumstances. Because we tend to pay close attention only to sickness, these healthy people have not received much attention, but my belief is that they manage to keep their lives under good control despite their circumstances.

Even in sickness, however, there is always the possibility that the old brain will come up with a newly reorganized behavior that will reverse what seemed a hopeless disease process. There are many recorded cases of miracle cures of late-stage, hopeless cancer patients. It is likely that these cancer victims' immune systems reorganized in such a beneficial way that they were able to act beyond their normal capabilities and eliminate the cancer. Reorganization can be miraculous, but it is not a miracle; it is a normal process in all living creatures.

In the brief time that most doctors spend discussing how well or badly people are living their lives, it is not easy to discover what in the patient's life is out of control. Before and even after his heart attack, Alan never felt right in complaining to his busy doctor about his high-paying job, so he said nothing. And it would have taken a skilled counselor to get him to reveal his strangle-the-boss fantasies, which might have led the counselor to help him realize the danger of these thoughts and guide him to a better way to handle his life.

In fact, it is quite characteristic of psychosomatic-disease sufferers that they tend to keep a stiff upper lip while they simmer inside with angering or some other controlling feeling behavior. If Alan had been a griper or complainer, he might have gained enough control through these feeling behaviors to protect his heart. But even if he had wanted to complain, he was making so much money that he would have found it difficult to get people to take him seriously and sympathize. I have had some personal experience with severe arthritics who, in superficial conversation, claim that nothing is seriously wrong with their lives except for the disruption caused by their disease. They seem to accept the destruction going on in their joints with a kind of calm resignation as if there is little they can do—it is all up to the doctor. What Norman Cousins' book *Anatomy of an Illness*[5] showed was how little a doctor can do and how much an arthritic can do for him or herself. I remember a talk I gave with Norman Cousins years ago, sponsored by UCLA, during which he spoke about his recovery from a serious form of arthritis. He described how he had checked himself out of the hospital and into a nice hotel room where he watched funny movies and laughed a lot. He also took mega doses of vitamin C. He took charge of his health and his pain.

But if you understand choice theory, this is exactly what you expect. People like Alan do not deal with their frustrations with the usual psychological new-brain feeling behaviors like angering, depressing, or complaining. For reasons that they may not even be aware of, they have chosen not to attempt to regain or take charge of their lives in the way most of us do. Instead, even with their disabling illnesses, they display such stoic cheer in their approach to the world that it is hard to suspect that there is probably something seriously wrong with their lives. While they appear to ignore their frustrations, their new brains are sending their old brain powerful help signals that lead to their diseases. But unaware of the turmoil in their old brains, they remain remarkably upbeat throughout their ordeals.

Sometimes, after they become ill, they learn to use their illnesses to gain control over others. I do not believe that this was in their minds before they got sick, but it could account for their cheerfulness—they are getting some payoff from pain and disability. This behavior not only tends to fool physicians but puzzles anyone who does not know choice theory. Physicians, especially, find it hard to believe that these seemingly mentally healthy, cheerful patients could have anything wrong psychologically. And the patients are almost always supportive of this stance. They hasten to agree with any doctor who treats them as unfortunate victims of a serious, completely physical disease.

Keep in mind that these patients have major investments in not choosing a feeling behavior to deal with their frustrations, because they are trying, for reasons known only to them, not to become aware that their lives are out of control. So, in a sense, physicians and patients join hands in denial of the cause of their illness and in doing so keep an important element, if not the most important element, of treatment—taking charge of their lives—out of the treatment picture. I am not claiming that good medical care is unnecessary, but medical care without better need-fulfilling behaviors will do little more than reduce the symptoms.

Cancer

As mysterious and frightening as cancer is to most of us, a great deal is already known about what causes a group of cells to reorganize and begin to follow its own genetic program. There is much medical speculation as to why this happens. External agents such as toxins, radiation, and some viruses have all been incriminated, and there is some evidence that internal agents, such as a cancer-causing gene (an oncogene) may play an important part in this first step. It is important to me as a psychiatrist to affirm that there is no evidence that the cellular changes leading to cancer are in any way psychologically caused.

It is a common observation in the medical community that some people, informed that they have cancer, seem to lose the will to live and die much more quickly than others with even more advanced disease. To the observer, it seems as if this new-brain knowledge causes some disruption in the immune system's normal old-brain instructions to fight the cancerous foreign invader. Even if we don't know that we have cancer, the old brain will still fight, even if it is fighting a losing battle. When patients are told they have cancer, some may just give up and say, "This is too much for me to handle."

When cancer cells have multiplied to the extent that there is a discoverable disease, we now believe the immune system has failed to function. For as yet unknown reasons, it either did not find the cancer cells or, if it found them, did not destroy them. In contrast to normal cells, which will multiply only a given number of times and then stop, cancer cells seem to be programmed for rapid and unlimited multiplication. They grow quickly and wildly and feed on normal body tissue. If unchecked, they will destroy the body with their overwhelming demands for sustenance. But we are rarely aware of this initial step, because we think that usually this growth is quickly and completely checked by our immune systems, which, if functioning normally, seek out and destroy these foreign cells before we are aware of their existence.

Some of our modern cancer treatments are aimed at augmenting the immune system to get it to function normally or even better. This type of treatment is very interesting to me as a psychiatrist because of the connection between mind and body, an area as yet little understood.

Life is not a static process. In the normal give-and-take of living, the old brain is constantly looking for creative new ways to help us to become healthier and better able to deal with disease. Cancer is a disease for which we need all the physiological creativity we can muster, and where we need this most is in the immune system. With cancer, the immune system is already not functioning as well as it should, and when we reduce or turn off its ability to be creative by sending it give-up hormones, we have little chance against cancer. We need all the new-brain resistance to giving up that we can transmit to the old brain so it will keep our immune systems as active and creative as possible.

The will to live is a new-brain behavior that may transmit activate-the-immune-system hormones to the old brain, the way Alan transmitted activate-the-fighting-system hormones to his old brain. What cancer sufferers who give up seem to do is just the opposite of what Alan did: in giving up, they might stop sending activating hormones, and the old brain and the immune system fail to seek a creative body solution to their problem. The behavior of giving up,

"What's the use of fighting anymore? I'm beaten," is often chosen when we are told we have cancer, the most dreaded of all diseases.

When we become aware that we have *any* serious illness, we are always hard pressed to retain control over our lives. We need all the help we can get at this point from everyone around us to retain the control that seems to be slipping away. But most importantly, we do not need to be put in any situation that is difficult for us to deal with. Every added difficulty is another obstacle, and tired and discouraged as we often are, the last things we need are more obstacles. For example, I believe that if I suspect that I may be suffering from a serious illness, such as cancer, I would not want to be told any more than was necessary for me to get good medical treatment. I would want to be told that there was a good chance I would get well, because there could be. I wouldn't want to see that my doctor was discouraged but that she would try her best for me. After that, I would not want to know anything more, because I would want to maintain as much control over my life as I could.

On my own, all I have going for me is my old brain and its immune system, and I know that the more I am in charge of my life, the better the relationship will be between my new brain and my old. And the better this relationship is, the more my old brain will fight creatively for my life. This fight may be as important to my survival, or at least to the quality of my remaining life, as anything my doctor can do for me.

Unfortunately, the medical practice of keeping still-functioning cancer patients in bed in large, frightening, impersonal hospitals is probably not sensible treatment. It is convenient for the doctor and hospital, but because much of the fight against cancer must come from within, it makes sense to keep our old brains as functional as possible. Anything that can be done to help sick people maintain control over their lives is probably an essential part of any good (old-brain-supportive) treatment plan. Most physicians recognize that this is true, but the whole thrust of scientific medicine with its awesome treatments and huge apparatus can present difficulties. By minimizing hospital stays, doctors seem to encourage patients to maintain control of their lives.

Everything done for (but really as much to) sick people in a modern hospital takes control away from them and puts it into outside hands. At some point, many patients begin to give up, because the little they are able to do gets them so little of the control they desire that continuing to fight is not worth it. Unlike Alan, they need to send fighting messenger hormones from their new brain to their old, and when they give up, they seem to stop sending these life-saving messages. The foundation of all good medical treatment, whatever the disease, should be to do as much as possible to help those who are sick maintain and even regain as much control over their lives as their disabilities allow.

9. Addicting Drugs: Chemical Control of Our Lives

There is a lot of controversy about whether addictions are psychological or the result of a disease process. This distinction is doubtless important and may provide ultimate answers to the cause of addiction, but as a practical matter, choice theory provides a workable approach to the management of addiction problems. From a choice theory point of view, addiction is a behavior based on addicts' belief that they must use some sort of substance to maintain control of their lives. To understand how addiction may work from a choice theory point of view, please take a moment to recall the last time you felt really wonderful. Wouldn't it be great if you could experience that same feeling right now? Unfortunately, you can't. To re-create that feeling, you must do something that gives you a powerful sense of control—fall in love, get a big promotion, win a big match, or escape from tyrannical oppression. Any sudden increase in love, power, fun, or freedom is always accompanied by a burst of pure pleasure, usually followed by a period of enjoyable activity. The act of eating or drinking a substance that acts on your brain might artificially give you that sense of control.

I have explained that our feelings are generated in two ways. Pure, short-lived, but extremely intense feelings occur whenever we are aware of a rapid increase or decrease in the difference between what we want and what we have. For example, we suffer pure pain when we hear that our good jobs are in jeopardy and enjoy a burst of pure pleasure when we find out that the rumor was false. However, the main source of our feelings, good and bad, is the feeling component of long-term behaviors. For example, we choose to depress for months as the best way to deal with losing a good job, or we choose the constant joy that goes with exciting, satisfying work.

The way we have evolved is that good feelings, both pure and long-term, are always a part of any effective, need-fulfilling behavior, like playing a good game of bridge or eating a delicious meal. Thus, we assume we are in charge of our lives when we feel good—and with one important exception, we are. The exception is when we choose to ingest, sniff, or inject addicting drugs. When drugs like heroin, alcohol, cocaine, and occasionally even marijuana reach our brains, we may, for a short time, feel ecstatic. The quick, intense pleasure that we experience feels very much like the pure, intense pleasure we feel when we suddenly take charge of our lives. When we feel this drug-induced burst of pleasure, we almost always fail to realize that even though we may feel ecstatic, our lives are always seriously out of control. If we continue to use any addicting drug, no matter how good we feel, we will always lose more and more control over our lives.

While good feelings are associated with effective control, I believe that control came first. You may observe simple organisms like plants struggling hard to stay alive—or in control—despite poor soil and hostile environments, but I doubt they have any feelings. Somehow, as higher animals struggled to fulfill their needs, feelings evolved: good feelings to reward them for succeeding in the struggle and bad feelings to warn them that needs were not being satisfied. And, of course, good feelings must be balanced by bad feelings or we would not recognize the difference between them. Knowing that bad feelings will be replaced by good feelings is also a powerful incentive to look for ways to regain control. We need the promise of the pot of gold at the end of our emotional rainbow to keep us moving in the right direction. When we have that pot in sight or in hand, we have every reason to believe we have taken charge of our lives.

Another difference between us and all other creatures is that we tend to be aware of the passage of time, and we relate this awareness to how well we are in charge of our lives. Time flies when we are satisfied and drags when we are not. When you are bored—for example, when your plane is delayed and you have to spend six hours wandering around an airport—you are not in control of your life, and the hands of the airport clock seem frozen. When you are in control, as when you are enjoying a wonderful vacation, the days fly by. You do all you can to prolong the experience, perhaps staying up all night with newfound friends, but still the clock moves with a vengeance, as if it has a personal vendetta to deprive you of as much vacation as it can.

When we are deeply involved intellectually, time flies. When I work on a project like this book, I can sit down in the early afternoon, and before I know it, it's dark outside. I don't feel any particular emotion—mostly my behavior is thinking—but still, as I make progress, time races by. So far as I know, there is no drug that provides this experience. The main addicting drugs, which I will introduce next, all give us a sense of control by providing a variety of pleasures, and because we feel so good, we tend to pay little attention to time. To do this, they act on the brain in the following ways.

Action One, Exemplified by the Opiates— Common Examples Are Codeine, Percodan, Morphine, and Heroin

All the opiates act on the brain directly to make us feel good. They imitate the recently discovered natural opiate-like chemicals secreted by our old brain, which provide most, if not all, the pure pleasure we feel when we suddenly take control in the real world. A golfer jumping for joy when he makes the winning putt is an example of how some people act when they experience the sudden secretion of a natural opiate.

The same feeling, perhaps even more powerful, is produced by an injection of heroin, especially if it is a large dose. Anyone using these drugs on a regular basis will become addicted, and while high will pay no attention to time. But when the addict runs short of the drug, time stands still, and few people are in less control of their lives than heroin addicts without access to their drug.

Action Two, Exemplified by Marijuana and LSD

Marijuana acts on sensory cameras by making the world appear easier and more pleasurable to deal with. It is a drug that seems to act as a mild pleasure filter in the back of the sensory camera so that what we perceive looks better, sounds better, tastes better, and feels better, and to this extent it is addicting. LSD also acts on our cameras but in a more powerful, unpredictable, and not always pleasurable way, so that people seeking control do not regularly use LSD. Drugs like LSD are used by people seeking new sensory experiences—perhaps a trip into a new world. It is common that while looking for the ultimate limits of experience, an LSD user perceives the world as so altered and distorted that he or she hallucinates. When this happens, the user may become terror stricken and correctly conclude that he or she has completely lost control. For this reason it is the rare person who becomes addicted to LSD. Its action is too unpredictable.

Action Three, Exemplified by Alcohol

More than any other drug, alcohol acts to give the user a quick and powerful sense of control. The good feeling that accompanies its use is how the user experiences this drug-induced increase in control. Unlike heroin and marijuana, which tend to render users passive, alcohol often leads its users to do something to increase the sense of control the drug has already provided. Under its influence and actually losing control, alcoholics may act as if whatever they do will increase the control they falsely believe they have. This action is unique; no other drug acts to increase a sense of control that is actually being lost. Bradley Smith et al., have been conducting research into choice theory interventions avnd alcohol consumption as related to self control on a college campus. Their research article states, "CT (choice theory) resonates with an informational tenor that does not confront the developmentally appropriate insistences on personal agency, self-interest, and autonomy typical of emergent adults"[6]

Action Four, Exemplified by Caffeine, Nicotine, and Cocaine

Cocaine and its weaker analogues—such as caffeine, nicotine, Dexedrine, and methamphetamine—also give a sense of control but in a different way. Their main actions are to energize the behavioral system so much that cocaine users, for example, can act for a while as if nothing is beyond their capabilities. Unlike alcohol, these drugs may for a short time actually provide the user with an increased ability to take control of his or her life. Obviously nicotine and caffeine are much less powerful than cocaine or methamphetamine, but they too are mild energizers and also seem to work well together. To verify this, ask anyone who uses both, to skip a cigarette or start a day with a cup of decaffeinated coffee.

Action Five, Exemplified by Barbiturates, and Valium

Unlike many of the previously mentioned drugs, these are mainly prescribed by physicians in an attempt to help tense patients relax and to assist patients who have trouble sleeping. They all act to sedate the behavioral system and in sufficient doses will produce a sleeplike state that is not nearly as restful as normal sleep. They do, however, produce a sense of pleasurable rest by reducing the urgency to behave in ways that may reduce our use of feeling behaviors like anxietying. All of these drugs are addictive if used frequently.

All regular users of addicting drugs can be said to be both psychologically and physically addicted. They are psychologically addicted because they become well aware of the pleasure the drugs provide and want to experience it as often and as long as possible. But they are also physically addicted in that the old brain accepts the drugs and integrates them into the normal body chemistry. Although we have no awareness of this because we have no direct awareness of any old-brain processes, the old brain learns that these drugs are beneficial to its functioning. We become aware that this has happened only when we try to stop taking the drugs. Then the old brain sends the new brain a pain message that we interpret consciously as a thirst for the drug. This is exactly analogous to the thirst for water or hunger for food.

It is this double benefit (mental and physical) that makes these drugs so addicting. But as the user increases the dosage in an effort to increase the pleasure, the old brain, unable to use that much drug, can no longer function satisfactorily, and the drug in effect becomes a painful poison. Unfortunately, as the user becomes poisoned by the drug, he or she tends to take more and more in a desperate attempt to feel better, producing the vicious, disabling, and at times even lethal action of these drugs.

If we stop taking a drug like morphine, cocaine, or Valium, it can take a very long time—up to several years—for the old brain to go back to its normal predrug functioning and forget the drug. During this interval we have little ability to feel good without the drug, because the old brain is inhibited from secreting the natural pleasure drugs that it normally secretes when we take effective control. This is a normal physiological process that always occurs when any natural drug or chemical is abundantly and regularly provided from the outside. Gradually the old brain resumes its normal function, but for a long time, the ex-user does not have the ability to feel natural pleasure and must struggle through a miserable period of joylessness as he or she waits for the old brain to begin secreting the natural pleasure drugs that we all need if we are to feel good.

This is why addicts complain so much about not having their drugs: they don't yet have the ability to experience the pleasures of normal living that nonusers take for granted. Alcohol is, of course, the exception, because it is not a natural pleasure drug. What it does is chemically provide a sense of control that the user cannot distinguish from effective need satisfaction. The intense pleasure alcoholics experience is a result of the action of their natural pleasure drugs, such as the endorphins that are always secreted when we suddenly gain the sense that we are in control. Therefore, an alcoholic who stops drinking and is able to satisfy his or her needs without alcohol has no difficulty feeling good—he or she has never interrupted this natural process.

The new brain, however, has an elephant-like memory for addicting drugs; nicotine, for example, may remain in our quality worlds forever. Although there may come a time when we no longer need the drug physically, we may never rid ourselves of the psychological longing for it unless what it provided is replaced by new effective behaviors. If we start to use the drug again, its chemical presence will quickly reactivate the old brain's memory, and driven by both a physical and a mental craving, we quickly become readdicted and once more lose the ability to secrete our natural pleasure drugs.

Stronger drugs like alcohol, cocaine, and Valium are also easily integrated into old-brain functioning and are perceived by the old brain as highly beneficial in small amounts. In the large amounts in which they are frequently used, they poison the old brain, and we become physically sick. But if we stop taking the drug, harmful as it was in the amounts we took it, the old brain continues for a long time, maybe for years, to send thirst messages to the new brain for the drug. It seems to have no way to learn that in large doses the drug is harmful; it remembers only the beneficial effects of the small doses, so no matter how poisonous, our old brain does not stop sending the get-me-some-drug messages to the new brain until it completely forgets. Therefore, if you want to quit any addicting drug, you have to depend on your new brain to come up with an effective need-satisfying behavior, such as succeeding at your work or reestablishing old family ties. The old brain, even if it has been repeatedly poisoned, will continue to crave the drug. And the stronger the drug, the longer this craving will last.

Marijuana seems to be a drug that is very easily integrated into old-brain functioning in the small amounts most users use it. It differs from most other addicting drugs, however, in that when we stop using it, the old brain gives it up easily. We seem not to get the strong old-brain thirst for it that we do for the other drugs. In small doses, therefore, it is more psychologically than physically addicting. In large doses, however, the old brain may grow to depend on it as it does other drugs, and it will also be physically addicting. In very large doses, it too will poison the old brain and lead to disturbed functioning similar to the perceptual disturbances caused by LSD.

Many people who use marijuana in large quantities will change to alcohol or other, stronger drugs because marijuana, even in large quantities, will not give them the sense of control for which they are searching.

It should be obvious to anyone who understands choice theory that addicting drugs, because they adversely affect both the old and new brains, are serious obstacles to taking charge of our lives unless used in small, well-controlled, social doses. Giving opium to starving children to prevent the pangs of hunger, a common practice in England in the time of Dickens, was hardly healthy; the first mild infection that came along was usually fatal to these victims of poverty. We have little starvation now but more drug use, because with affluence, we have become more aware that pleasure is possible. Addicts seek it incessantly and don't hesitate to use drugs if they can't get pleasure easily any other way. Even if you don't use drugs to excess, it is valuable, because of their widespread use, to know how they affect those around you. The following information is not intended to be a treatise on drug rehabilitation. It may, however, be of great value if you have to cope with drug users when they are under the influence and should get you started if they ask you for help to stop using.

10. Common Addicting Drugs, Legal and Illegal

Alcohol

The most dangerous and debilitating of all the common drugs is alcohol, partly because of the way it acts upon us but mostly because its heavy use is so socially accepted that we tend to disregard the well-known fact that when it is used in large amounts, it almost always leads to disaster for the user.

Alcohol is an extremely simple compound, but no one has yet discovered how it works in the body to give almost all users a powerful belief that they are in control of their lives when actually they are not. This effect is cumulative: The more they drink, the greater the sense of control they experience. I have many friends and colleagues now in Alcoholics Anonymous who drank for years, and they confirm that this is the major effect. The picture that they successfully pursued was drinking until they felt in total control, which meant until they were drunk. But actually, the more alcohol they consumed, the less control they had. The common characteristic of all drunken alcoholics is the vast difference between the amount of control they actually have (almost none) and the amount of control they believe they have (total).

It does not seem to matter which of the several needs is not fulfilled; alcohol gives the user the false sense that it is. It makes the lonely sociable, the powerless powerful, the gloomy fun-filled, and the imprisoned less confined. And since our society is filled with people who are unsatisfied with the way they are choosing to live their lives, many use alcohol in huge quantities. As mentioned earlier, unlike heroin or cocaine, it does not give pleasure directly but from the satisfying sense of control, which probably causes a concurrent liberation of the drinker's own natural pleasure chemicals—the internal opiates.

For the user, whether the pleasure is direct or indirect is only a technical point; the pleasure felt is immediate and intense. The technical point is important in the rehabilitation process, however, because the alcoholic never loses his ability to secrete natural pleasure drugs. Once he stops drinking and regains control, he can feel good almost immediately, so there is great incentive to stop drinking if he can retain control without alcohol. He does not have to wait the long interval without pleasure while his own natural pleasure drugs are reactivated, an interval that almost always occurs when a direct pleasure drug like heroin or Valium is withdrawn.

As the years go by, even the most obtuse drinker begins to become aware that the control he feels when drunk has no substance in fact. He cannot escape from the sickness and disability that are a part of his life, drunk and sober. He cannot fool himself into believing his needs are satisfied when everyone around him turns away and he is left alone. Still he does not quit and may even drink more because he has taken everything except alcohol out of his quality world. So he drinks alone, depending totally on the drug and even giving up trying to do the things he used to do incompetently when he believed alcohol made him competent. This continued use of alcohol, common among the residents of any city's skid row, is less to get pleasure and more to become unconscious. Only with loss of consciousness can he escape from the painful sense that, even drunk, he is still far from in control.

The most insidious action of alcohol is that the user has no perception that he has lost control until the drug begins to wear off. Without the drug, he feels a huge burst of pure pain that always accompanies the immediate loss of control. So as soon as he can, he drinks again, each time fooling himself into believing that he has finally gained control. He also believes that anything he does while under the influence enhances that control. This crazy belief that what he does is good for him and, unfortunately, for those around him (remember he thinks he is in control and does not realize he is drunk) leads to the most destructive aspect of alcohol—violence. Many violent crimes, especially the wife and child beating and the incestuous relationships that are so much a part of our culture, are a direct consequence of drinking. The countless but less premeditated tragedies of drunk driving, boating, or flying far outnumber the accidents that occur when the operators are sober. Alcohol consumption is one of the prime causes of violence—intentional or unintentional—in our society, and it is more often than not the motivator for sexual abuse by men of women and children.

There is a common scenario of a drinking man—we'll call him Mack—whose marriage is rapidly deteriorating. Each day as the alcohol takes effect, he believes that he is in control and can now do anything he wants, and that his wife—we'll call her Kay—will not only go along with it but will like it and like him as he does it. Perhaps he just makes a simple demand that she go out and get him some more beer or a more complicated demand that she have sex in a way that she does not like, or at least not when he is drunk. She may refuse to get the beer or participate enthusiastically in the sex. His false sense of control is as repugnant to her as his drunkenness. She may have started this evening like many others by asking him to drink less—which he bitterly resents. All day long he has looked forward to his evening beer and to the control he regains with it.

To Mack, sobriety is the misery and pain of an out-of-control life. Kay's nagging represents all the control he does not have, and alcohol represents all he longs for. Because alcohol is the greatest of all rationalizers, Mack, when drunk, thinks that anything he does is justified. Having lost all the ability to judge what he does with any accuracy, he "knows" he is in control; no one has a right to dispute his authority, and if they do, he is going to do what he believes necessary, with no thought that what he does may be horribly violent. When Kay refuses to get him more beer, he beats her, because she has no right to challenge a man who is in control. Drunk, he is the captain of the family ship, with the right to put down any mutiny—and he does.

Kay, not knowing choice theory, does not know what is going on. She cannot possibly grasp the fact that he believes he is in control, because it is so obvious to her that he is not. She believes that she is doing him a favor by refusing to get him beer and expects he will have some ability to realize this, but of course he does not. The alcohol has given him confidence that whatever he does is effective, and he may beat her severely, believing it his duty as a husband to straighten her out.

All this takes place slowly. In the beginning, when Mack got a little tipsy, it was fun to be with him, because he gained confidence in himself. And with the better sense of humor and the mild feeling of power the alcohol gave him, he related better to Kay. If he had never drunk past that level, as social drinkers do not, the sense of control that the alcohol gave him would have made him more attractive and easier to get along with. When we have confidence, we are better for having it, and this is the seemingly sensible rationale for using alcohol.

The problem that all drinkers face is to maintain the delicate balance between just enough and too much. But as any drinker gains confidence, he also tends to lose the ability to stop at the point where this mild confidence is attractive and helpful. He is tempted to take another drink, especially when he is a little out of control from a hard day or a brush with his wife or kids. First Mack went a little past that level; then a lot; and finally, instead of trying to work out problems, he drank to work them out chemically. The vicious drinking cycle was established. He only feels in control when he is drunk, because when he is sober, Kay does not miss an opportunity to tell him in a thousand ways how dreadful he has become to live with. Theirs is the typical alcoholic marriage: she is in control when he is sober; he is in control when drunk. Without help, neither will be able to patch up the differences between them.

Kay stays with him for the usual reasons—love, loyalty, security, children—but one reason common to most wives of alcoholics is that as time passes, she has more and more control over him when he is sober. This compensates somewhat for the violent control he takes when he is drunk. If she cannot learn what is going on, all she can look forward to is more of the beatings and less sobriety. As long as she does not realize that drinking gives him a sense of control, she has no way to deal effectively with him. She will continue to badger him when he is sober, and he will drink more and more to regain control. But if she can manage to stay alive, she will win. The poisonous effect of alcohol will eventually make him so sick that he will surrender to her care. He will lose the physical stamina that he needs to keep drinking in quantity, and she will be left with a shell of a man—a burned-out, sick drunk.

If Kay wants to take effective charge of her life and marriage, there is much she can do to put what is explained here into practice. First, she must learn that Mack drinks to gain the control that he has lost. And when he is drunk, he feels justified in doing anything to regain his lost control, including violence. She must make a plan to leave the house when he starts drinking, and if she has children, to take them with her, and not return until he is sober. If on some occasions she can't leave, to protect herself and her children, she must not thwart him. He may see even a tiny crying baby as a threat to his drunken control, and to him it may make sense to beat an infant.

She should also learn that there is no way that she can, by herself, reform an alcoholic. When he is sober, he may listen as she tells him about the terror and confusion he creates when he is drunk, but all this does is cause him to further lose control and yearn for more alcohol. Her good intentions—and his when sober—unfortunately compound the problem. Mack has lost control of his life, but Kay is so intimately involved in this loss that she cannot help him. It is impossible. He must stop drinking, and in my work with alcoholics I have learned that he will not stop until he gets into an Alcoholics Anonymous program that will help him begin to regain control of his life without alcohol. Kay must learn the hard lesson that she can control her own life; she cannot control Mack's. If she continues to try, she may be killed.

If she wants to begin to control her life, she must decide whether she wants to control badly enough to continue her life of accepting drunken beatings and listening to guilty promises to stop. If she decides that this is not what she wants, she must tell him while he is sober that she cannot and will not continue to live with him as they are. If she understands what I have just explained, she will realize that life with Mack will get worse, not better. As a condition of her staying with him, he must go to AA, or any recognized, relationship based intervention and/or treatment program. To deal with her problems, which she must admit to him that she has too, she will get involved with Al-Anon, the AA program to help families of alcoholics. In fact, she should tell him she will go to Al-Anon whether he goes to AA or not.

What she will learn in Al-Anon—a program that, like AA, follows choice theory—is how to live with him in a way that allows them both to feel as if they are in control of their lives and their marriage. If she can't learn this, her only chance is to get divorced. If she is strong but not damning of his drinking or of him and tells him that they can't stay together while he continues to drink, and if there is anything left of their marriage, he will go to AA. There he will learn that he has lost control of his life but can regain it without the need for alcohol. He will change the picture in his quality world from alcohol to AA. She will change her picture from controlling him to caring without control, and they will have a chance. There is no other; alcohol is too powerful. AA is the only program that I know of that helps alcoholics consistently and without cost. But even AA is not the total answer. It is the beginning, the chance to get sober. While sober, the alcoholic must regain enough control over his life to satisfy his needs. AA by itself cannot satisfy all his needs, but it is a way—probably the best way we have available—to get the process started.

Alcohol is so much a part of our culture that it is sometimes difficult for a nondrinker to gain social acceptance. Anyone who does not drink has to be strong enough to find friends who accept him or her as a nondrinker. This is not hard for successful adults; but for teenagers, because they have such a pressing need for acceptance as they make the transition into adulthood, not to drink is to risk being left out. Besides, most see and experience drinking in their homes, and sometimes a little drunkenness is treated by the family more as a joke than as a potentially serious problem.

I believe that alcohol will always be an integral, accepted, even glorified part of our culture, while other drugs will not, because alcohol is supportive of the cultural ideal—taking control of your life. The fact that alcohol is the single most destructive force in our culture that causes people to lose control is not recognized and will not be recognized, because of how it acts. The culture, or at least the culture presented by mass media, sees it as a positive force, which it may be if it is used in delicate moderation. Supported by the media, our culture falsely assumes that real men and women will not exceed the very fine line between enhancing and losing control. Alcohol is the get-things-done, take-control drug, and to deal with it well is a sign of strength and maturity. Because it enhances the sense of control, we welcome it instead of fearing it as we should.

The advertised image of beer links it with hard, exciting work and athletic accomplishment. People who are really in charge of their lives drink a lot of beer on TV and never lose control. If you believe the ads, the work is always done well; the drinking is never on the job or while playing the game; the parties are always fun; and no one ever gets into an accident driving home. Alcohol is advertised as the drug that happy and successful people use, and they never lose control when they use it. So when a young person begins to drink, he or she rarely considers how fine the line is between moderation and drunkenness—just one too many, and a life may be irreparably damaged or lost. And of course the young user never feels out of control, because the more he uses, the more in control he thinks he is. Long after he is a confirmed alcoholic, he continues to believe he is just like the people in the ads.

The way a parent can help a child deal with this insidious and dangerous drug is to stay on good terms with the child and, if the parent does drink, to do it in moderation as a model of how to handle alcohol. Talking to a son or daughter and explaining the effect of alcohol and the fine line between moderation and excess is also wise. Trying to persuade a son or daughter to go to AA is, to me, a must for any parent who knows that the child has a drinking problem. Don't be fooled into thinking a child is too young to be an alcoholic; children as young as ten years are regular members of AA meetings. Parents of alcoholics should attend Al-Anon, and brothers and sisters of young alcoholics should attend Alateen, a special program for teenagers who have family members attending AA. But the most effective thing we can do is try to raise our children so that they are enough in charge of their lives that a chemical sense of control is less needed. In a later chapter I will summarize how parents might best use knowledge of choice theory to raise more effective children.

Desperate parents and other family members should also be aware that curing alcoholism and abuse of other drugs—especially cocaine and prescription drugs—is big business. The daily newspapers are filled with ads offering hope that is likely not a reality. Many of these (often ineffective) programs are unbelievably expensive, and since some of them are covered by medical insurance, their widespread use has greatly increased the cost of this expensive insurance for all of us. Anyone thinking of getting involved with a profit-making drug program should investigate very carefully what is being offered for the money. Many are no more than custodial: personnel are untrained, the doctor is more on the letterhead than an active participant, and the addicting drugs that they are supposed to be treating are available for a price. What is mostly sold is temporary relief for the family by getting the addict out of the house, and if you buy this, you are compounding the problem, not treating it.

There are also many legitimate low-cost programs available that can be located via the internet, such as the Alcoholism Council website, www.alcoholismcouncil.org. Regardless of cost, before you enroll anyone in a program, especially a live-in program, you should get the names of at least three people who have completed the program and have been drug-free for a year. You should talk to these people; they will not only be willing to talk to you, they will want to talk to you. This is the only way you can find out what you need to know about any program. If anyone offering a program is not willing or able to provide you with these names, have nothing to do with that program.

Marijuana

No matter what I write about marijuana, many will disagree. If I call it a dangerous drug, many users will point out that it hasn't harmed them. How do they know? You can't use and not use at the same time, so you have no way of knowing how much better or worse you would be without the drug. But if I call it a mild pleasure drug, many nonusers and the anti-marijuana lobby will criticize me and show me research proving it causes everything from psychosis to birth defects. Fortunately, my purpose is not to resolve this controversy but to try to make some sense out of this drug's action, to explain how this particular drug misleads people into believing that with it, they are in better control of their lives.

Any drug that is used to cause pleasure or kill time is dangerous, and marijuana is in that category. It is also a potentially addicting drug, but it has flaws that make it much less addicting than alcohol and most of the other pleasure drugs. Marijuana does not give much of a sense of control. Nor does it energize, sedate, or produce much pure pleasure. It is more widely used than all drugs except alcohol and caffeine, but it is less abused, because like caffeine and nicotine, its effect is not particularly enhanced by high doses.

Its major effect is to make the world seem easier to control by causing whatever we deal with to appear more pleasant. Unlike alcohol users, marijuana users are more tolerant of the world. They do not have the urge to take control by action and become passive, bemused observers of the struggles of those around them. Since our get-up-and-go culture lauds action and frowns on passive observation or any passive pleasures, those with power in our competitive culture consider marijuana more dangerous than alcohol because a marijuana user tends to drop out rather than compete. Alcoholics may get drunk, sick, and disabled, but for a long time they are competitive, and to that extent the culture supports their efforts. Marijuana is an anticulture drug because it renders its users passive and accepting of the status quo. Chronic users have little motivation to pursue the work ethic of our culture.

Those who must do boring work argue that marijuana makes the work less tedious and their drab jobs more endurable. If used frequently, however, it will impair both the workers' ability and desire to do a good job. People whose lives are seriously out of control will find little satisfaction in marijuana; it can't make an unloving spouse loving or an unsatisfying job satisfying. When those who use it find this out, they often turn to stronger, more controlling drugs, especially alcohol, because it is legal and accepted. Those whose lives are under relatively good control may stay with marijuana and even prefer it to alcohol, but like social drinkers, they tend not to use it excessively.

Even in small amounts, marijuana tends to reduce incentive and motivation to struggle hard, and its users often settle for less than their potential. Though they may recognize this effect, under its influence they do not care to do much about it. This is what worries parents whose children smoke marijuana, and it is a legitimate worry. But how can a parent persuade a child to stop using or, even better, never start using this drug? A good relationship with the child is probably the parent's best weapon. No parent can completely control the child's activity, but it is reasonable for parents to insist that children do not smoke marijuana in their house. Most children will respect the wishes of a parent whom they love and respect and will adhere to this rule. And because it is a drug that children like to use at home, they may thus use less.

Parents should avoid using their good relationships with their children to persuade them to replace dangerous marijuana with safe alcohol. The effort should be to try to get them to live a drug-free life, not to get them to move on to what, for them, may be an even more dangerous drug. But I have no great words of wisdom here. Children who feel they are in charge of their lives will not use any drug to excess. If you have a good relationship with your child, and if the child is successful in what he or she does and has learned that hard work leads to success and pleasure, you need not worry if the child uses marijuana or alcohol in moderation. Moderation is measured by how well the child is in control of his or her life. If the child is not in control, is not happy, has few friends and few or no active interests, and does not do well in school, that unhappy child is likely to begin using pleasure drugs, usually beginning with alcohol or marijuana. These are the unhappy facts of life in the twenty-first century.

Heroin and Other Opiates

For centuries, users of opium and its stronger derivatives, such as morphine and heroin, have suspected that there is a special quality to these intensely pleasurable drugs. Then, in 1975, scientists discovered what this special quality is: these drugs mimic a natural heroin-like chemical that is secreted in our bodies whenever we feel pleasure. While many people find the idea that we secrete heroin in our bodies disturbing and hard to accept, the facts are clear that we do.

Whether we like it or not, when we gain control of any situation, we feel good because our bodies have secreted their own natural heroin, giving us a small shot of pure chemical pleasure. The addict uses large doses of heroin, probably far beyond what we normally secrete even under the best of circumstances, in an effort not only to mimic but to exceed natural pleasure experiences.

Addicts are not interested in doing anything to gain control of their lives except to inject heroin. This is because with heroin they are in control, supreme control, and they experience the pure pleasure that comes with total control. A heroin addict doesn't care if his wife won't go out for a beer or have sex with him or even if she leaves him forever. All he cares about is the feeling of heroin, and when he is high, he is withdrawn and not hostile.

Most people who turn to heroin do so because their lives are very much out of control, and they quickly become addicted. Neither I nor anyone else has any wisdom for heroin addicts. They have found what they believe all people are looking for, and they are satisfied. Without heroin, as they suffer withdrawal, they are about as out of control as a human being can get. But most of them are driven hard enough by the withdrawal or the fear of it to figure out how to get heroin. The need of the addict is so intense that even in many prisons heroin is available to addicts who can pay for it. Many lose their lives with impure drugs or die of illnesses associated with long-term use and the physical deprivation that accompanies it.

Some give it up through the use of powerful group programs, but most stay with it for a long time. There is reason to believe that many finally give it up on their own, because those who work with addicts report that they almost never deal with people over forty-five years old. They can't all be dead, so the solution to this mystery of where they go or what they do must be that they get tired of the rat race that accompanies the daily struggle to finance their habit and stop using the drug. Possibly many of them turn to always-available alcohol. The picture is not bright. Heroin is a life-destroying drug. Few people who become addicted to it are able to resume a normal life without the drug either on their own or with the help of others.

The Uppers: Caffeine, Nicotine, Benzedrine, Methamphetamine, Cocaine, and Other Synthetic Stimulants

When the German armies waged the blitzkrieg or lightning war through France and the Lowlands in 1940, the Allied forces were no match for their stamina and ferocity. The Germans fought like men possessed, and they were. Their pharmacists had synthesized methamphetamine, a cheap but powerful energizing drug that allowed their soldiers to fight vigorously for weeks at a time with no sleep and little food. Just as the Indians of the high Andes can perform prodigious feats of strength and endurance while chewing the coca leaf—from which they get cocaine and other energizers—the Germans fought like demons stoked with cheap and readily available methamphetamine. Like horses doped for a race, they did not fight fairly, but fairness is a concept that has no relationship to modern war. The British used methamphetamine widely during World War II, and the Americans distributed Benzedrine to pilots in the European theater and a few years later made use of methamphetamine in the Korean War. For short-term use, before the user is drained, these drugs do provide prodigious amounts of energy.

The uppers, ranging from mild (caffeine and nicotine) to powerful (cocaine), are among the most addicting of all drugs. They energize the behavioral system so that it performs better—a little better for caffeine and nicotine and a lot better for Benzedrine, methamphetamine, and cocaine. But even a mild energizer like nicotine quickly becomes so much a part of our regular body chemistry that once it is accepted, the body needs it to function. Anyone who has smoked for the length of time that most people smoke before they consider quitting knows how much the body begins to hurt when its nicotine is removed. Mild as it is, nicotine is considered as addicting as any drug, because we use it for so long that even the old brain seems never to forget it. Caffeine is similar, but the effect is milder, and the old brain will forget it much more easily and quickly than it does nicotine.

Caffeine seems to do us little physical harm, but nicotine is both directly and indirectly harmful. It seems directly linked in some way to predisposing us to heart disease, and indirectly, through the tars that we inhale when we smoke, to lung cancer. It is, however, the tars, not the nicotine, that are carcinogenic. There also may be a psychological relationship between nicotine and heart disease in that those who do not smoke are probably in better control of their lives and thus less likely to have any psychosomatic disease.

The powerful energizers are cocaine and its synthetic analogues—methamphetamine, Benzedrine, and Dexedrine. In sufficient doses, these give such an unbelievable rush of energy that those who use them in large doses feel that if they wanted, they could take over the world. Feeling this way, they enjoy a temporary increase in the performance of simple physical tasks, such as fighting or having sex. If the task is complex and requires more than just energy, they probably do not perform very well. But regardless of the performance, what they do in all cases is drive their behavioral systems far beyond their normal capacity to function without rest.

All biologic systems need time for rest, renewal of used-up chemicals, and excretion of waste products. But for users of cocaine or methamphetamine, there is no rest. It never ceases to drive, and behavioral systems driven by it invariably start to become creative in a desperate effort to continue to perform at higher and higher levels. Ultimately, the user turns almost completely to his or her reorganization system and begins to think crazy thoughts and do crazy things. I believe that even the reorganization system is somehow affected by these drugs, and it becomes more chaotic and biased toward weird, frightening hallucinations like worms crawling out of the skin.

Until relatively recently, these drugs were not considered addicting, because they led to craziness, and with craziness the drug is necessarily discontinued. The user becomes so crazy he or she does not even know he or she is taking the drugs, but to think that they are not addictive because of this is wrong. Cocaine may be the most addicting drug available, because people who are normally in good control of their lives—successful athletes, performers, and high-flying business people—seem to be susceptible to it. They all seem to be seeking more energetic performance from their behavioral systems, and for this they seek cocaine. This is a different population from the more passive seekers of intense pleasure who use heroin, the go-with-the-flow marijuana users, or the nonperforming-but-think-they-are-performing alcoholics.

It is possible that some people can use these drugs in moderation for the lift they provide, but because they are so addicting, this is difficult to do. Very quickly the drug takes over their lives and users lose all control, including the control they need in order to continue to use in moderation. As they become enervated by their constant activity and exhausted by their inability to sleep, they may try heroin or alcohol in a desperate effort to get some chemical rest. But these drugs do not provide rest, and in the failing effort to find it, users may become addicted to them and vastly compound their problems.

Again, I have no words of wisdom except to beware of treatment programs that offer a cure for huge sums of money. Talk to some successful graduates before you mortgage the house for a promise that may not be fulfilled. Of course, these drugs have to be flushed out of the body. That's easy if the addict gets into a program where the drug is not made available for a price. What is difficult is to flush them from the old brain and the new brain's memories. To get users to forget and start living their lives without the drug, a program must be long-term, starting with a drug-free environment for many months and maybe even a year. This must be followed by an intensive outpatient counseling program in which the patient's blood or urine is checked regularly for the drug for at least twice as long as the inpatient program or longer. It is wise to beware of slick ads promoting programs that promise easy or quick cures. Such cures do not exist.

The Addicting Drugs That Doctors Prescribe

Addicting drugs have legitimate medical uses and can be an aid to taking effective control in diseases, but caution in this use is important. We live in a world where we all believe that what ails us is caused by something outside of us, so we tend to believe that the cure is also outside—if we are sick, the drug can cure us. But by now you have learned that most pain and sickness are related to our losing effective control of our lives, and while doctors can help, it is our responsibility to augment that help by regaining the control we have lost. Knowing this, the doctor's most important responsibility becomes to avoid any treatment that will make it more difficult for us to regain control—or at least to retain the limited control we may still have. Any doctor who gives us a pleasure drug and does not make sure that we use this drug for a limited time only while we gather ourselves together and regain control is doing us no good and much potential harm.

There is sense, even mercy, in a doctor's giving chemical relief to patients who are choosing to suffer because their lives are out of control—but only if at the same time they use the temporary relief the drug provides to get the counseling needed to regain control of their lives. To give any addicting drug without offering to help the patient get good counseling and without following through to see that the patient is acting on this advice is medicine at its worst. Doctors do not need to help people lose control of their lives; they do this well enough on their own.

Sleeping pills are one of the most abused prescription drugs. They are given to people who do not have enough control over their lives to accept that, while a period of sleeplessness may be uncomfortable, it is not dangerous to health. All of us will eventually sleep enough for our needs, but if we take pills we do not sleep normally—and to be healthy, we need normal sleep. Abnormal sleep may be more debilitating than insufficient normal sleep.

It is commonly accepted that normal sleep entails a necessary amount of dreaming. Medications for sleeping cause us to be unconscious but disrupt the normal and necessary nightly access to reorganization that is dreaming. We need dreams to resolve and bring under control the small but constant frustrations of the previous day. Without our creative dreams, we wake up hung over, still wrestling with what our dreams would have resolved. And because we are not rested, we find it even harder to cope. Now we need our normal dreaming sleep even more but find it even harder to relax enough to go to sleep. If we then take more sleeping medication, as many do, we become addicted and dig ourselves deeper and deeper into a state of constant exhaustion. Then, to function better when awake or to stay awake, we use too much caffeine, nicotine, or even stronger drugs—legal and illegal—and find it harder and harder both to sleep and to function while awake.

There is no drug that can produce the normal sleep we need to get the rest that gives us the energy to maintain control over our lives. In fact:

There is no long-term benefit from any addicting drug, legal or illegal, no matter how it acts.

But there is tremendous profit in both legal and illegal drugs, so they will be pushed on us from all sides as panaceas for pain, misery, exhaustion, and being overweight. It is up to each of us to protect ourselves by refusing to use any addicting drug for more than a short time. We cannot depend on anyone else to do this for us.

A large number of legally prescribed antipsychotic and antidepressant drugs are in wide use today. It is a widely accepted medical theory that psychosis and depression are diseases caused by some chemical imbalance or disruption in the brain, just as diabetes is caused by the failure of the pancreas to produce sufficient insulin. Certainly, if we examined all psychotic and depressed people carefully, we would find that out of the millions who suffer, there are a few whose psychosis or depression is caused by some chemical abnormality. In these rare instances, their lives are under control; it is their old-brain chemistry that has gone haywire. This is supported by the fact that some—diagnosed as bipolor, that is—of the many people who alternate between mania and depressing, benefit dramatically from a drug called lithium carbonate. They seem to be people whose lives are under control when they are in the normal phase between the mood swings. These people, however, are far fewer in number than those who are given lithium in the vain hope that this chemical will cure them.

Neither I nor anyone else knows the numbers exactly, but my long experience tells me that there are probably ten thousand to twenty thousand people who depress because their lives are out of control for every one who is depressed because of a primary chemical imbalance. Nevertheless, huge quantities of antidepressant and antipsychotic drugs are prescribed in the vain hope that they will cure a nonexistent disease. Again, used in small doses as temporary relief until patients can be counseled to regain control over their lives, these drugs have benefit; but used to cure, they promise a hope that they cannot fulfill and are a cruel delusion to patients and the patients' families.

Antipsychotic drugs act to paralyze the whole behavioral system so that it cannot be creative—or, in these instances, crazy—but unfortunately the system also can barely behave at all. Under the influence of these strong drugs, patients are like zombies. Their ability to be spontaneous is gone, and if the dose is large, they can barely walk or talk. The most serious sign of the harmful effects of these drugs is that all joy in life is gone—patients who use them cannot even laugh. While these patients are no longer crazy, they are really not alive enough to gain the control they need to get back to any normal existence.

Antidepressant drugs are not much better if used for more than a short time. Their action is to activate our own internal, natural energizers, but to do so these strong drugs disrupt so much essential body chemistry that they are disabling to the user. For example, they can interfere with mental clarity, digestion, and normal sleep. And after a while, patients who do not receive counseling and whose best choice therefore is still to depress will again depress so strongly that they will override even large doses of these drugs. At this point, the drugs are either so ineffective or so disabling that patients can no longer tolerate them.

No drug can fulfill our needs. To do this, we must regain control over our lives. If we need good counseling, we should get it, but even without counseling there is much that most of us can do to regain control if we understand choice theory and use it in our lives. We cannot depend on others to provide us with choices, and we absolutely cannot depend on long-term use of drugs to do anything except get in the way of our regaining the need-fulfilling control that is the only answer to our problems.

11. Conflict

Can you imagine going to work on Monday and finding out that your new boss has ordered that anyone who wants to keep his or her job must work Saturday? That's the day your son's team plays for the championship, and he's pitching. You've waited through a long season for this big day, and your son, assuming you'll be there, talks of nothing else. As you listen to his excited chatter, you can't get up the nerve to tell him you may miss the game, and inside you feel as if you are being torn apart. What you are experiencing is the almost total loss of control that comes from the destructive effect of conflict on your own system. You have a powerful urge to do something—but what? There is no behavior that can put you in two places at the same time, so you depress all week long in an effort to soften the blow if you decide to miss the game.

It's as if your house were designed to maintain a steady 70 degrees but with two thermostats instead of one. The first thermostat is hooked to powerful cooling systems set at 60, the second to an equally powerful furnace set at 80. Both go full blast all day long, and the house indeed hovers at 70 as long as they keep going, but eventually one or both will break down from overwork. No sane engineer would design such a system; it would not make sense. But when you are in conflict, you are suffering from the living equivalent of such a faulty design. There is nothing to prevent us from wanting to satisfy two totally conflicting pictures at the same time, fully aware that it is not possible.

In another example, Jeff is offered a huge promotion on the basis of his moving across the country to open a Boston branch office, but his wife, Kelly, who is an only child, tells him she will not leave her aged parents on the West Coast. When he tells this to his boss, he is given three months to make up his mind. If he turns down this opportunity, he doesn't think he will ever again be considered for anything this good, and he is eager to make the move.

To express this conflict in choice theory terms, Jeff has a picture in his head of moving to Boston and being his own boss, but he also has a picture of a loved wife who will not consider such a move at this time. She told him when they married that she would not leave San Francisco as long as her parents were alive. She is perfectly satisfied with what he earns now and has faith that if he stays put, things will still somehow work out.

Jeff is caught between satisfying his needs for power and freedom and his need for love. He can't talk to Kelly about how torn apart he feels, because, not sharing his conflict, she is not sympathetic. He continues to talk to his boss about the problem, but his boss counters with how many times he and his wife moved so that he could get to where he is. If Jeff isn't going to go, his boss urges him to make the decision quickly so they can look for someone else.

To consider another conflict, let's look at Helen. Unlike Jeff, her conflicts are not between conflicting needs but between two aspects of the same need. She is torn between her love for Bill, the man she has lived with for months, and her love for her two children. Bill no longer wants to share her with her children, and he has given her an ultimatum: send them back to their father (who wants them) or he will move out. If she wants both (and having close friends who have both, she does not feel that what she wants is unreasonable), what can she do?

Most serious conflicts evolve from our attempts to control others who will not accept our control because what we want does not satisfy them. If Kelly would go to Boston, Jeff would do all he could to make it possible for her to spend time with her parents—even move them to Boston. He is willing to be more than reasonable and will extend himself to see that her life is disrupted as little as possible, but she will not discuss the move. She does point out that she is the beneficiary of a substantial insurance policy and that when her father, who is in his eighties, dies, they will be financially independent. She refuses to see that he does not want her father's money but the power and self-esteem he will get from the new job.

For the short time he has lived with her, Helen has insulated Bill from her children in every way that she can, but he is still adamant. He wants her but no children that are not theirs. He admits they are good children and is willing to have them for a few weeks a year but not on a permanent basis. He claims he is not selfish and just knows himself and his limitations. Helen begs him to try it for a while longer, but he refuses. He tries to be reasonable, telling her it would not be fair to anyone for him to pretend to accept her children when he feels he can't.

Like the two conflicting thermostats on the wall, Jeff and Helen continue to experience a substantial difference between what they want and what they are able to get. They are in what is best defined as a true conflict, because neither of them can come up with a single behavior that can satisfy both of their pictures. As a result, like the furnace or air conditioner, their behavioral systems are going full blast all the time. Still, no matter what they do, there is always a difference between what they have and what they want.

But remember, as long as we drive our behavioral systems, they never stop producing behaviors; and when we are in conflict, no matter what we do, there is always a difference between what we want and what we have. As it attempts to reduce this difference, the behavioral system continues trying to come up with a satisfactory behavior; it has no ability to recognize that the task is impossible. This is why, when we are in conflict, no matter how much we realize there is nothing we can do, we feel a continuous urge to behave. As it desperately searches for a satisfactory behavior, the behavioral system becomes more and more creative. Jeff has begun to reorganize physically through the common (but new to him) behavior of chest paining. He has consulted physicians, but none can find anything wrong with his heart. Helen has begun to reorganize with compulsive housecleaning and has also chosen to become obsessive in the discipline of her children in a vain attempt to prove to Bill that they will be no problem. After working all day, she cleans half the night. She is drinking twenty cups of coffee a day to keep going and taking Valium in the early-morning hours in an effort to get some sleep. Caught between conflicting desires, both Helen and Jeff have lost control of their lives.

Conflict is among the most common causes of long-term severe suffering, because nowhere do we lose more control than when we are in a true conflict. Jeff may push himself from chest paining to true heart disease, and Helen may turn to drugs far stronger than caffeine and Valium, but if neither Kelly nor Bill will budge, the conflict will remain. True conflicts like these are not common. Much more frequently we tend to get ourselves into situations that seem to us to be true conflicts but are not.

In these more common situations, best called false conflicts, there is always a single behavior that will resolve the conflict, but this is also a behavior that the person who complains of conflict is rarely willing to use. For example, Gert wants to be a size ten, but she also doesn't like to leave the dinner table hungry. She is willing to skip breakfast and eat a tiny lunch, but at night, after a hard day's work, she wants a full meal and eats one. She is thirty pounds over what she would like to weigh and complains of her conflict every time she shops for clothes and every night when she sits down to dinner. She believes she is caught between conflicting desires when, in fact, with some effort she could have both.

This is a false conflict because if Gert were willing to run four to five miles a day, she could be a size ten and still eat a substantial dinner. Besides burning calories, running also seems to make people less hungry, so food becomes less important. The problem with this perfect solution is that running four miles a day is hard and takes a lot of time. Many people would rather blame being overweight on their conflict than do the hard work that would allow them to have almost all the food they want.

False conflicts abound. We all know people who agonize about how much they would like to go to college but say they can't because they have to work or people who go on about how much they would like to get out of the house and go to work but say they can't because of the children. These are difficult situations, but none is a true conflict. In every case, if the conflicted complainers were willing to figure out a tough course of action and put it into practice, they would have a good chance to get most, if not all, of what they want.

In every false conflict there is an obvious hard-work choice that the conflicted person does not want to face. It is not easy to work a full-time job and go to college, but millions do. And many more figure out how to take care of a house and family and work full-time. When confronted with the hard-work alternative, some argue that they don't have the physical stamina. But they will never know unless they try. We all have a lot more strength than we realize if we can get involved in doing what we want to do.

Staying in a loveless marriage for security or because the children need a mother or father or some variation on this theme is another common false conflict. If you are willing to do the hard work that making a change will require, there is almost always a way. Assuming you have done all you can to find love in the marriage, choosing to stand pat is almost always tantamount to choosing a life of self-imposed misery. Even staying with a man or woman who won't marry you and trying to convince yourself that he or she is committed is usually little more than unwillingness to make the effort to find someone who wants you enough to marry you.

We should also be aware that people often use the complaint of conflict to control us. For example, Jack complains to Gwen—and sometimes to his wife—that he is caught between his loyalty to his wife and family and his mad, passionate desire for Gwen, the other woman. Jack, however, is not in conflict at all; he is using the screen of conflict to control Gwen and maybe also his wife so he can continue to have his cake and eat it too. If Gwen or his wife learns basic choice theory, they will stop buying into his conflict, and then Jack may be faced with a real conflict. As long as the others accept the story of his torment, he has them under good control.

Because most of us do not understand how different a true conflict is from a false conflict, we tend to deal with both of these situations badly. What we do is exactly the opposite of what is effective: we treat conflicts as if hard work will resolve them (it won't) and false conflicts as if there is nothing we can do when there almost always is. For example, Jeff, who is in a true conflict, believes that if he works hard on a persuasion program, he can talk Kelly into going to Boston with him. But if she won't go, he is helpless; he cannot force her to change the picture in her head, which is to stay in San Francisco.

What makes a true conflict so disastrous is not only the fact that there is no solution but that there is no respite from trying to find a solution.

Both Jeff and Helen continue to try for the impossible because their behavioral systems are being continuously driven by strong signals. In Jeff's case, he wants Kelly and the move; in Helen's case, she wants Bill and her kids. There is always a large difference between the picture they want and what they have. The only way they can save themselves from the misery and self-destruction they are already choosing is to learn that in the case of a true conflict, the best behavior is to consciously and with complete awareness of what one is doing choose to be passive—do nothing to attempt to resolve the conflict.

While doing nothing active is simple to advise someone, it is terribly difficult to practice. Doing nothing, while certainly a legitimate behavior is also the most passive, and therefore the most difficult to choose when the urge to behave is powerful. The only way that someone in conflict can actually do nothing is if he or she understands the choice theory basis of conflict that I have just explained. With this understanding, doing nothing is a logical behavior—in fact, it is the only behavior that makes any sense when we are in true conflict. Jeff cannot be in San Francisco and Boston at the same time, and Helen cannot have both Bill and the children, so why try? We may be up against a stone wall, but we don't have to bloody our heads against it unless we choose to.

To better understand why doing nothing is the best choice, picture yourself in the middle of a large room with a door on the wall to your left and another on the wall to your right. Behind one door is a large pot of gold; behind the other is the lover of your dreams. Both will wait for you quite a while, and there is more time than you think; the urgency is more in your head than in the situation itself. If you try to force yourself to decide, as you move toward one door or the other, you will find yourself pulled back to the center of the room by the invisible string that is your desire not to lose what is behind the other door. You strain first one way and then the other, expending a lot of energy but getting nowhere. Wouldn't it be more sensible, since there is no immediate need to choose, to sit down and wait as comfortably as you can in the middle? If the situation changes while you are patiently waiting, as any situation might in time, you may be more able to make a choice. If you wait and a choice does seem to present itself, you will be much less exhausted and more able to deal with what you choose.

If in the end either Kelly or Bill relents, Jeff and Helen, who have waited patiently, will be better able to work things out than if they were exhausted from being miserable, sick, tired, alcoholic, or crazy. When waiting is possible, the longer you wait before you make a decision, the more likely it is that time and events over which you have little control will help you make up your mind. The world never stands still. Things tend to happen that no one can predict, and the conflict unbalances. If, while Jeff waits, he continues to work hard and is gracious to all concerned, Kelly's aged parents may tell Kelly that she should go with Jeff, or the company may decide to offer him something else close to home. The boss may be replaced or get sick and suggest that Jeff take his job. Another company in San Francisco may find out that he is a top-notch worker and make him a better offer. Any or all of these events over which Jeff has little control would resolve the conflict. What he has control over is the decision to wait and do a good job while waiting.

Helen's calm but resolute love for both her children and Bill may cause him to relent. Or her former husband may change his mind and refuse to take the kids. It is unlikely that her situation can remain the way it is for very long. As long as Bill only threatens but gives no final ultimatum, she has to assume that, even with her kids, he may need her more than he has expressed so far. If she continues to love him but makes no move to get rid of her children, there is a good chance that things will work out for her. She has control over her life, so she can wait.

We should never underestimate the value of doing nothing as effectively as we can when we are in true conflict.

The problem with waiting is that there is usually a lot of outside pressure on us to *do* something. If we discuss our dilemmas with others—and most of us do—they usually urge us to make a move. We must keep in mind that it is only to us that our conflicting pictures are equal, so the pressure friends put on us to act is always from their much less conflicted standpoint, never ours. We tend to resist this pressure, but this uses valuable energy. We would be better off without their advice, but to avoid this advice, we have to stop asking them what to do. If all we want is sympathy and reassurance, then talking about our predicament is helpful. But it is foolish to look to others for solutions—they have none.

Because waiting is so hard and the urge to move so strong, a good way to make the waiting easier is to try to spend as much energy as you can satisfying yourself in an unconflicted area. Since none of us can do more than one thing at a time, Helen might satisfy her urge to do something by working hard on her job, spending more fun time with her kids, exercising and getting into good shape, and doing some of the gourmet cooking that she has always wanted to do. Do anything that moves you in any satisfying direction that is not involved with the conflict and you will be in more control of your life. And the more you are in control, the less torn apart you will feel even if the conflict takes a very long time to resolve.

If you find that the urge to do something active is so strong that doing nothing is impossible, then you can put time to work for you instead of against you as it may seem to be working now. Tell yourself that you will try either one side or the other for a specific length of time and then see how things work out. This gives you an element of control that you just don't have while waiting and doing nothing. For example, Jeff might decide that he will go to Boston by himself for six months and see what happens. He may or may not tell Kelly about the six-month time element depending on his judgment of what she may or may not do if she knows. In his mind, however, it is a six-month trial, and during that time a lot could happen to resolve the conflict.

Helen could tell Bill that she has made up her mind that she is not going to give up her kids. She will continue to treat him with a lot of warmth and no complaints, but she can't accept his conditions. Instead of waiting for him to give her an ultimatum, she gives him one. She has decided to give him six months to make up his mind, but whether or not she tells him about the time limit is up to her. She takes a chance that he will leave, but in this way she gains a little more control over the situation.

If you decide to make an arbitrary move for a period of time, you still have to pick which way to go. You might take a piece of paper, divide it in half, and head each column with a choice. In Jeff's case, one column would be headed Boston and the other San Francisco. Write down a Boston reason and then a San Francisco reason and go back and forth listing reasons until you can't think of any more. Whichever side has the most reasons, go that way for the time you have chosen. Few conflicts are exactly equal, and this way you may find which picture is the best to try. If making this decision becomes another conflict, however, this solution is not for you. It would be better to do nothing and wait.

Difficult as it is to do nothing when we are truly conflicted, the opposite occurs when we are in a false conflict—here we find it easy to do very little except complain. It is easier to moan about how we lack willpower while lapping up hot fudge sundaes than to run the four miles a day that could make them possible. Seeking sympathy because your kids need you so much that you can't go back to college may mean you would rather talk about what you want than work to get it. In time, most true conflicts resolve or move toward resolution, but false conflicts seem to get worse. It will be a lot easier to start running when you are ten pounds overweight than thirty.

If you believe you are conflicted, it is important to learn how to determine whether the conflict you are struggling with is true or false. To do this, take a look at the conflicting pictures you want and try your best to figure out if there is a single behavior (consider the hard ones too) that will satisfy both. If you take a long, honest look and find that there is none, then you are in true conflict, and rather than choose to tear yourself up, attempt the passive waiting strategies suggested in this chapter. If, however, you are in a false conflict, face the fact that what you want is obtainable only through hard work and start working. Both hoping and complaining are among our least effective behaviors.

Of all creatures, we are the only ones who suffer significant conflict and therefore the only ones who have developed systems of morality as part of our attempt to resolve this conflict. Simple creatures like clams or snails have no conflict; all they want is to stay alive and reproduce. Even complicated animals like apes suffer little conflict, because they do not have our driving need for power and our long-term need for committed love. However, because we suffer conflict and are always looking for the way out, we are almost always very concerned with morality and responsibility or how to fulfill our needs without depriving others of a chance to fulfill theirs. The problem we continually face in practice is that it is very difficult to be responsible or to make the moral and responsible choice, but who is to say whether staying in San Francisco or going to Boston is more responsible? Is Helen irresponsible if she sends her children to her former husband and settles down alone with Bill?

While it is easy for others who are not in the conflict to preach morality and responsibility when you turn to them for advice, what may be obvious to them is far from obvious to you. Has Kelly more responsibility to her father and mother than to her husband? Is Jeff being responsible to himself if he gives up the promotion he wants so much? If we want to take charge of our lives, we must face the fact that there will never be a standard morality we can depend on to guide us when we are in true conflict. In fact, the test of a true conflict is that we can make a good moral argument for either side. Therefore, when we are in true conflict, as much as we feel driven to turn to others, even moral authorities like judges or ministers can no better direct us than a flip of a coin.

Some might argue that when a conflict is between power and love, it is more moral to opt for love. But where does this argument lead when the conflict is within the love need itself—as illustrated by Helen, who is torn between love for her children and love for her fiancé? Should she give her children to her former husband, who wants them, and marry Bill (remember, these are his terms for marriage) or keep them and give Bill up? In this situation, the advice that Helen would almost certainly get would be to chuck Bill; her prime responsibility is to her children. This appears to be morally sound advice, but if Helen takes it and then misses Bill, she may anger and take this anger out on her kids or turn to drinking and neglect them; in either case they might be better off with their father. Still, there is a good rationale for the standard moral position, and that rationale is loyalty: all other things being about equal, the old takes precedence over the new.

In the same way, Jeff is likely to be advised by many that the older loyalties of Kelly to her parents and his to Kelly should take precedence over the more recent promotion. Counter to this argument is the fact that Jeff may have been ambitious long before he met Kelly and loyalty to his ambition should not be disregarded. But sticking to the old as long as you can is not only moral, it is also effective in that it almost always buys you more time. As I have explained, in time most conflicts tend to become resolvable, so here the loyal choice is not only a little easier in that it usually is supported by those around you but also turns out to be practical.

Here's another example. Jud gave Paul his first job more than twenty years ago, and now Paul has risen over Jud to the presidency of the company. Jud, who has a serious drinking problem, is still in middle management. Over the past five years, while Paul was a vice president, he protected Jud out of loyalty to the man who gave him his start. Jud is now totally incompetent, and without Paul's protection he would be fired. His drinking has come to the attention of the chairman of the board, and Paul, the new president, is in a quandary about how much longer he can protect a man who is a long-term liability to the company. There is no doubt that an old loyalty is being tested, and Jud throws himself on Paul's mercy when Paul calls him in to talk about what Jud must do—stop drinking—but never does.

You might argue that we do not owe loyalty to an incompetent drunk, but are the ethics of loyalty such that we need only be loyal to the innocent or presently competent? That would be a hard standard for judging our friends.

As long as there is no conflict, there is rarely a serious moral problem; loyalty will work well as a basis for most moral decisions. But when conflict enters the picture, whether it is within a need or between needs, there is no standard moral position that will work for the conflicted person. When you are being torn by a true conflict, you must recognize that, for the moment, your morality will not work. It is this recognition that will help you to retain some control over your life and not feel as if you have lost control because you are immoral. To attempt to regain control by trying to force yourself in one direction or another through guilting and depressing will not help. Keep in mind that if there were a succinct moral solution you would not be in conflict in the first place. People who consider themselves moral and loyal might advise Paul to say to Jud, "I have done all I can for you for five years; now it is up to you to sink or swim." These people have limits to their loyalty. Paul either has no such limits or has not reached them yet with Jud.

When you practice loyalty and it works, you are fortunate, but you should be wary of preaching it because it worked for you. It worked mostly because it gave you time, or possibly because you were not in a true conflict—you only thought you were. It is especially unpleasant to be lectured to by someone who claims that he or she has suffered a true conflict exactly like yours and solved it through moral willpower when, in fact, he or she was not conflicted at all and resolved nothing that was not easy to resolve.

We must face the fact that as long as we have conflicting needs or as long as our individual needs can be satisfied in conflicting ways, we will always have true conflict. Morality may help us in time, but at any conflicted moment it may give us little relief. We must accept that no one can walk in our shoes except ourselves, and only we can decide what is best to do. The most valuable choice theory principle in this most difficult of all situations is to choose to wait, to delay the decision as long as we can. Every day of delay gives the situation time to evolve, and in its natural evolution the right or moral choice may become clear. But it will become clear only as the situation changes; if it does not change, there is no solution, easy or hard. When Saturday comes and your employer won't relent and give you time off to go to the game, whatever you choose will be a painful choice. There is no way to avoid the pain. It is the human condition—the price we pay for the complex genetic instructions that have carried us to the top rung of the evolutionary ladder.

We must be aware that there is no rule that says the pictures in our quality worlds must never conflict. They do more often than not. But there is also no rule that says we have to try to satisfy conflicting pictures at the same time. We must keep in mind that these are our pictures—we put them in, and we can choose which of them we want at any time. Helen does not have to love Bill; she is choosing to love him, knowing that he rejects her children. Jeff does not have to take the Boston job; he is choosing to satisfy his need for power in this way at this time. We have some control over which pictures we want from our quality worlds, and if we learn anything from choice theory, it should be to give careful thought to wanting something that is in direct conflict with something else we want.

Conflict is an inevitable part of life and is always difficult to resolve. What may help us is to keep in mind that …

We will not help ourselves or anyone else involved in a conflict if we choose to immobilize ourselves with pain and disability.

The rationale for all courses of action suggested in this chapter is that, difficult as they may be, they are more effective than misery.

12. Criticism

Take a close look at any good relationship—husband-wife, parent-child, teacher-pupil, employer-employee—and you will see that what makes the relationship work is caring, respect, and mutual goals. As important as these are, what is even more important to a relationship's success is what you won't see: criticism. Any lasting relationship, whether equal like husband-wife or unequal like teacher-pupil, has continued more because the people in the relationship don't criticize each other than because they share a lot in common.

By now, you are well aware that to gain control over our lives, we need to get along well with those close to us. When we do, our lives are filled with pleasure. Most of us, however, experience the most difficulty getting along with those closest to us, members of our families. This is because we criticize them the most and they do the same to us. Most families live knee-deep in criticism, with little awareness of how totally destructive this is to their getting along. The more intimate the relationship—and marriage starts out as the most intimate of all relationships—the more destructive criticism is to its success.

Verbal criticism can take the form of sarcasm, ridicule, and hyperbole. Over the centuries we have developed countless ploys to put each other down. Because we are so relieved that it is not happening to us, criticism is the source of much humor. *The Bickersons*, about a couple that bickered and criticized without mercy, was a hit on radio for years in the 1930s. Don Rickles, a popular comic in his day, made a lot of money criticizing defenseless celebrities whom, because of their accomplishments, he considered fair game for his barbs, and our laughter showed that we agreed.

But criticism is much more than what we say; it is looking at each other with disgust, disdain, or even hatred. It can also consist as much of what we don't do—and make a point not to do—as of what we do or say. When we turn away or won't talk or listen, we tell others they are worthless to us; for example, when someone is talking, to make a point of not listening, to act in his or her presence as if he or she is not there. Verbal or nonverbal criticism is rude and painful.

Not only do we criticize each other far too much, but many of us extol the virtue of this behavior, calling what we do constructive. What to me is constructive criticism is almost always regarded by you as a put-down. If you grant that I am smarter, you lose power and tend to resent me and my help rather than listening seriously to what I offer. Only in situations where you believe your needs will be met by bowing to my superior wisdom, and only if you respect and care for me as a person, will you listen to me when I criticize you. Young children, students, and newly hired workers may take constructive criticism in the spirit it is offered, but even they, as they assert their need for power by asking for more equality, will grow resentful of too much unsolicited help. This is why modern managers use seminars and workshops to teach new techniques: people will accept instruction from an occasional outside expert much more readily than from someone they know. "A prophet is without honor in his own country," because there he is seen more as a competitor than a teacher.

Because of our pressing need for power, even thoughtful and gentle criticism between equals or people striving for equality will not work. As we attempt, constructively or not, to improve the people we need, both we and they lose, rather than gain, more and more control over our lives. Still, destructive as this is, we are well aware of what we are doing when we criticize. Until you make choice theory an integral part of your life, you may, for example, find it hard to accept that you choose to depress or to headache. But there is not one of you who could convince anyone, including yourself, that you do not choose to criticize those with whom you live and work. Almost all of us pay a bitter price in lost relationships because we constantly let those around us know that what is good for them is to perform the way we picture them in our quality worlds.

You may recall that Susan was highly critical of Dave for leaving her for another woman. It is unlikely that this was the first time she had criticized him. My guess, based on the many marriages I have seen fail, is that not only Dave but Susan too was highly dissatisfied with their marriage long before he left. I would guess that both of them engaged in a great deal of personal and perhaps bitter criticism of each other long before the break. Whatever else the woman for whom Dave left Susan did, it is likely that early in their relationship she was as accepting of him as Susan was critical. It is doubtful that she is still noncritical now that they are married. Indeed, if Dave were to make overtures to Susan to return, my guess would be that this new marriage had reached a level of criticism that exceeded what he had with Susan.

I do not want to imply that Susan was wrong to criticize Dave. She did what all of us do who do not know choice theory. She was trying what she knew best to correct what she believed was wrong with her marriage. Dave was not perfect—none of us are—but he probably would have been a much better husband if she had used a more effective behavior than criticizing him for his flaws. Before I go into what she might have done that would have been a more effective choice, let me try to explain why criticism is so destructive to relationships.

Choice theory teaches that any relationship—for example, Dave and Susan's marriage—is really two relationships. Dave's marriage is a picture in his head, and Susan's a picture in hers. The success of their marriage depends on keeping the marriage they have in the real world close to these pictures in their heads. When either Dave or Susan became aware that there was a substantial difference between the marriage he or she wanted and the marriage he or she had, they had no choice but to attempt to reduce this difference. To do this, each chose the only behavior most married people know—criticizing the other for not living up to that picture. Driven by our need for power, we choose to criticize in an attempt to force the other party to accept our view of the relationship.

If Dave had taken Susan's criticism in the spirit in which it was offered and changed his ways, there would have been no problem. He didn't, because what she wanted was not what he wanted; no husband and wife have the exact same marriage in their quality worlds. When her criticism failed to change him, she angered, depressed, and withdrew, and both their marriages got worse. As these painful feeling behaviors failed to control Dave, whom she felt was slipping away, her increased criticism probably was the final blow to an already shaky marriage.

What makes criticism so destructive is that there is nothing else we do that will so suddenly and painfully make the criticized parties acutely aware that there are huge differences between them.

Faced with this difference, few marriages survive. All do not end in divorce—many couples continue to live together—but the marriage is essentially over.

The best way to explain how criticism causes this sudden huge difference, which almost always leads to destructive feeling behaviors, is to carry this example further and, for the sake of illustration, make it somewhat extreme. Suppose Dave had taken Susan on a winter skiing weekend while they still had a semblance of a marriage. He loves to ski; she likes it when conditions are perfect, which they rarely are. He promised that he had checked things out carefully—the season was right for good weather, and the accommodations were supposed to be first-class. When they arrived, it was great for a day, and then a blizzard snowed them in for a week. The accommodations were okay for skiing but inadequate for being snowed in. They got a little cabin fever, one thing led to another, and she may have said, "This always happens—your stupid plans always go wrong. How could I be such an idiot as to let you plan anything? The only thing you'll ever plan well is my funeral!"

Just writing this hypothetical outburst is painful to me, but in my profession this is mild compared to what I have frequently heard. I am sure that as you think through your own experiences with criticism, you can match or exceed the discomfort of this example on both the giving and receiving end.

Dave too was hardly enjoying the week's imprisonment, and now, as Susan impugned his competence in every area, they had difficulty avoiding blows. They didn't speak to each other for a week—and later, when Dave told the other woman what Susan had done to him, she assured him she would have been delighted to be snowed in. They would have made love for a week and had a marvelous time. It does not take too many incidents like this to push a failing marriage over the brink.

When people are important to us, we continually compare them with the pictures we have of them in our quality worlds. Ordinarily, if we get along well, the pictures we want are not far from what we have. If at times they frustrate us, we can avoid a lot of misery if we don't criticize. For example, if Susan asks Dave to stop at the store on his way home and he forgets, as he often does, she might ask him if he would make a special trip now as she needs the tomato sauce for tonight's pasta. He's tired, doesn't want to go to the store, and hates being reminded that he is forgetful, but because there was no criticism in her reasonable request, he grumbles and asks her if she really needs it. She says she does, and he goes. If either had said something critical, they might have had a blowup.

Criticism, therefore, is much more than just finding the world to be different from the way we want it. It is the world turning against us and telling us that what we want is senseless, stupid, or without value. For example, if I ask you to do me a favor, I may choose to be unhappy if you refuse, but if you tell me I am a fool for asking or that what I want is stupid, it is likely I will lose all control. What I will almost always do in a desperate effort to regain control is anger, because angering is the behavior we all tend to choose when we feel the world is suddenly and (usually) unexpectedly out of control. Nothing we encounter leads to a greater and quicker loss of control than being criticized. And it is harder to regain control when we are criticized than in any other situation.

In my opinion, criticizing is by far the single most destructive behavior we use as we attempt to take charge of our lives.

Tired as he was, Dave had no problem with Susan asking him to go back to the store because there was nothing in this reasonable request to put him down. This situation is much different from what happened in the ski lodge, when he was blamed for everything, including the blizzard. People who have studied choice theory extensively believe that almost all the synapses in the brain—literally billions of them—are involved in the process of comparing the pictures we have in our quality worlds with what we see in the real world. When we are criticized, the sudden huge difference in the pictures occurring in all these places feels as if the whole brain is exploding in pure pain. Simultaneously, we feel an immediate and overwhelming urge to behave. This urge is so strong that even our usual angering often seems insufficient, and we quickly turn to our creative systems for new behaviors, which are often more violent or painful than we have ever chosen before. If the person being criticized is under the influence of alcohol (see chapter 10), the potential for violence is greatly increased.

I believe some sort of personal put-down is involved in most violent behavior directed at others or at ourselves that occurs within families and among friends. It is well known that regardless of how unsafe our streets may be, more than 80 percent of all homicides are committed by people who know each other well. When severe criticism occurs, the painful explosion in the brain and the huge concurrent signal to behave drives too many of us to irrational angering in an attempt to regain control at any cost. Caesar fought heroically until Brutus, his beloved friend, struck. Then, impaled by criticism as much as by the blade, Caesar gave up. If we can become aware of the extent to which criticism is always associated with severe loss of control, we will make an effort to learn to deal more effectively with frustration in our relationships.

Criticism is a luxury I believe none of us can afford.

Everyone is familiar with at least one couple who got along together before they married—and maybe even lived together amicably for several years—whose relationship mysteriously deteriorated after the marriage. The solution to the mystery is that many husbands or wives regard the marriage license as a license to criticize. This same license seems to be an unfortunate part of most long-term close relationships, as if the length of the relationship has made it strong enough to survive critical correction. This is exactly the opposite of what we should do. If criticism is ever effective, it is in the beginning of a relationship when the person being criticized may not feel equal to the criticizer and may accept some constructive correction. As any relationship matures, the parties involved tend to move toward a feeling of equality, and criticism is resented more and more. I believe it is from the long-term custom of criticizing those close to us that the saying "familiarity breeds contempt" has come into our culture. Unfortunately, as we grow more and more familiar, we believe that it is not only a right but a duty to tell people close to us, constructively of course, how badly they are doing and how much better off they would be if they did it our way.

Perhaps the most insidious form of criticism is self-criticism. If you criticize me, I can usually get away from you. But where can I go if I criticize myself? In my quality world I always picture myself, whatever I may do, as competent. It does not matter to me that you may think my behavior is incompetent. Like a decision to roll in the cacti, it is my best present effort to fulfill my needs. As I look at how I deal with the world to satisfy these pictures, I realize that I am often unable to get what I want for myself. My guess is that Susan, now that Dave has left and married someone else, spends part of her time reviling herself for not doing more to preserve the marriage. What she is doing is punishing herself for what she may have done wrong, and the more she does this, the less competent she will be to find the new relationships she needs. She may have done many things wrong in her marriage (Dave did as many or more than she did), but what effective purpose does her self-criticism serve? If it taught her to be more competent in her next relationship, it would serve a purpose, but angering and depressing do little more than sap her strength.

The more we flagellate ourselves with brutal self-criticism, the more we increase the difference between what we see and what we want for ourselves. To deal with this increase, we usually choose to depress, use alcohol, or contemplate suicide as we move toward choosing creative behaviors. If we want to keep control over our lives, we must not only learn to avoid criticizing others, we must equally avoid criticizing ourselves. I live by a helpful little motto: "I won't criticize myself—there are more than enough people willing to do it for me."

If, however, I see my spouse or child doing something wrong, am I supposed to stand by and say nothing? How are they, especially children, to learn if no one makes the effort to point out what they are doing wrong and show them how to correct it? Of course I have to say something, but what I say to children up to age twelve or thirteen will be different from how I will deal with older children and adults. Young children still look to parents for instruction. They know that they need guidance, and they are not yet engaged in the power struggle that they will join shortly. All I need to do is tell or show them a better way and pay little attention to what they had been doing that was wrong. I can also use this constructive approach with adults if they view me as a teacher or are not in competition with me.

If I attempt to use this same constructive approach with someone who is in any sort of a power struggle with me (as are most of the teenagers and adults who are close to me) that person will construe even mild correction as criticism. For example, as good as my intentions are, when I tell my grown son that he would be better off flying to San Francisco than driving, what he hears is a personal put-down. He hears me accusing him of inadequacy or bad judgment and becomes frustrated so quickly that he tends not to listen to the constructive reasons for my opinion. As adults, we are so competitive, so busy maintaining our power, that we rarely listen to what is often sound advice. The basic flaw of criticism, therefore, is not that it isn't well intended but that its intentions are almost never realized. Instead of helping people to function together more effectively, it almost always drives a wedge between them.

What I would like to suggest is a way to correct people—especially those close to us—that will not drive them away. In fact, if we do it properly, we may even bring them closer to us. For example, when Susan was snowed in, to maintain some control she looked around for someone to blame. There were only two people possible: she and Dave. She chose to blame Dave and did it in a devastatingly critical way, driving nail after nail into the coffin of their marriage. Choice theory would suggest that she say to Dave, "This is going to be a rough week if we are going to be snowed in. I know you don't like it, and neither do I, so how can we make the most of this time?"

This way she does not blame him and does not cause him to lose control. But she is still dissatisfied, so she could also say, "Even though I know it's not your fault, I still find myself getting mad at you. Maybe we should talk about the fact that there are things I like to do and things you like to do, and they are not always the same things. You like to go to the snow a lot more than I do, so when you want to be skiing, let's talk it over and figure out what I could do when you're gone. You really have more fun by yourself."

She could use the time while they are stuck in the cabin to work out a plan for the future instead of working on the destruction of their marriage.

The general rule that I am suggesting is that when you want to correct someone, do it by saying, "Let's take a look and see what is and is not working for me, for you, and for both of us. This means taking a good look at my picture, your picture, and the situation." You may not be able to agree on exactly what the situation really is, but you do know whether it is working for you, and the other party knows the same. Then go ahead and try to work out a plan that will work better for both of you than what you have now.

For example, your employee is not doing the job, and you want better performance. Following the above, you do not criticize, but you call him in and say, "I want to take a look at what we are both doing in this situation to see where it is working and where it isn't." Of course he will tense up, but stick to the situation and go through what both of you did on a recent day (yesterday is best) step by step. Point out what you think you did and ask him to point out what he thinks he did. If you don't agree, then talk about where you see things differently, but don't get involved with whether or not what you don't agree on is good or bad. The most important thing is to move on until you agree on something you both could do that might be better. Then work out a plan to try it, set a schedule to check, and, if necessary, revise the plan. Listen to him—you may learn a new procedure that is valuable. He is unlikely to say that everything he does is good; more likely, he will point to the areas that need improving. If he sees nothing that needs improving, then take only one area and explain that this is an area in which you believe he could show improvement. Ask him for suggestions on what he might consider doing to improve his job performance in that area. Point out what you would be willing to do that might support his performance.

This last suggestion is close to constructive criticism, but the difference is that in this scenario, you do not point out the performance problem, you give the employee a chance to recognize his own problem. This approach will work to start the process of change, even for a resisting employee who admits to no weaknesses when you see many. As soon as he sees that you are more interested in finding a better way than in criticizing, he will begin to find other flaws, because he will get the idea that you are trying to build him up, not tear him down. The real key is to make a joint evaluation of the situation and try to correct it cooperatively so that it works better for both parties. If you do this both with your family and in your work, you will find that your life becomes much better. This way not only does no one lose control but both have a chance to get even more. Following this method, there is little need to criticize.

Reward and punishment, the external motivators our culture reveres, are so closely related to criticism that it seems sensible to discuss them here. Like criticism, both are products of stimulus-response psychology and would have little utility in a world that followed choice theory. A choice theory world would be well aware that our only motivator is the pictures we pursue from our quality worlds and that what happens outside of us does not cause us to do what we do. Reward and punishment are based on the false idea that people can be forced or persuaded from the outside to do what they do not want to do. Most of the institutions in our society attempt to motivate with reward and punishment, and this is an important reason why many are breaking down, especially our schools, our heavy industries, and our families.

Praise, on the other hand, can be a good motivator if it satisfies our need to belong and if it is adapted to the situation. If it is not spontaneous and does not vary with performance, then it is in the category of a reward and has much less value.

What is wrong with both reward and punishment is that they interfere with the individual's perception of being in control.

If I punish you to get you to do what I want, then I am your controller, and you will resist what I do because you lose some control. But even if I reward you, as much as you may like the reward, you will know you received it because you did what I wanted, and you may still resent my control. Certainly we would rather be rewarded than punished, but if you think the reward you receive is intended to manipulate you, you will choose to resent it. Even with my reward in hand, you have surrendered a degree of control to me and you don't like it. This resistance to control can help explain the dynamics of some labor-management negotiations, for instance in the coal-mining industry. In this industry, strikes are almost always long, even though the basic wage issues are not irresolvable. Coal miners do a hard, dangerous job, and when they strike they are interested in a sense of control through recognition as well as a monetary reward.

We are all motivated by the basic needs and feel good when we fulfill them. The best praise I can imagine is for you to rejoice with me. But for you to get me to do anything you want, you have to show me how it satisfies me. Most of us work hard for money because we want the control that money buys, but the picture of money is already in our heads when we go to work. If you can persuade me that there are other rewards for working hard, I may work for these as much as for money, but first I must put these rewards into my quality world—you cannot put them in for me. A boss who gives spontaneous praise for good work may get more work from his or her employees than one who pays well but never praises.

Stimulus-response psychology works on the premise that the rewarder or the punisher knows what the responder wants, how much of it he or she wants, and how often he or she wants it. None of us knows enough about the pictures in another person's head to guess any of these things correctly on a consistent basis. This is why most stimulators eventually resort to punishment: they know that none of us (masochists excluded) has a picture of being hurt as a need-satisfying picture. Pain, therefore, is a strong motivator for getting us to do simple manual tasks for a while. If the task is complex, however, the person threatened with punishment will figure out a way to mess up the work and avoid blame. Slaves dig ditches; they don't program computers. In time, however, no matter how great the pain, most of us will refuse consciously (by deciding death is better than compliance) or unconsciously (through getting sick or crazy) to do what does not satisfy us. This is why, for complex tasks and creative work, no one in his or her right mind would advocate a chain gang as a good way to get the job done.

Our stimulus-response management approach to production has been significantly outperformed by the Japanese, who use choice theory management based on a great deal of communication with workers and continually upgrading the work to keep it as need-satisfying as possible. They depend neither on rigid rewards nor on threats of layoffs to motivate people to do the complex jobs demanded by modern technology. Ultimately, any system that depends exclusively on external motivation will break down. Nowhere do we see this breakdown more clearly than in our public educational system. Schools are rife with criticism, failure, and rigid reward and punishment in the form of grades.

So far all the remedies for the schools are based almost exclusively on stimulus-response psychology—longer school days, harder projects, tougher grading standards, and increased failure for nonperformers. We hear little of the need to persuade students that learning is need-fulfilling so that they will put the idea of education and the hard work necessary to learn, into their quality worlds. Choice theory education is possible. It is successfully practiced in a few schools and in quite a few industries, but it will never become widespread until it becomes a part of our culture. It is paradoxical that as much as they practice choice theory in business management, Japanese schools are much more dominated by stimulus-response psychology than ours. The intense competition to succeed and the punitive disgrace of not succeeding are so powerful in their schools that the whole nation has become concerned with the rash of suicides among students who have failed to achieve the high standards of the pictures in their heads.

13. Taking Charge of Your Life

Using Susan, who had marriage difficulties, as an example, I would like to explain how we can put choice theory to work in our lives when we find ourselves losing control of a situation. If Susan had known choice theory, as soon as she became dissatisfied with her marriage, she would have taken an honest look at the behaviors she was choosing for dealing with her frustrations. She would have seen that she was engaging in a lot of criticism of Dave and herself. She would have become aware that, except for short bursts of angering, she was almost always depressing as she desperately tried to get more love and attention from Dave. As soon as she realized that she was choosing her misery, she would have asked herself the important choice theory question, "Is the criticizing and misery I am now choosing helping me to get what I want?"

The answer to this basic question, which must be asked by anyone who wants to regain control of her life, is always no. Choosing long-term pain or criticism is not going to get us what we want now or ever. Choice theory not only gives us the ability to recognize that we choose our behavior and that we may be making bad choices but also clearly states that as much as we may want someone to change, all we can do is attempt to gain better control over our own lives.

We have no power to make others do, think, or feel anything that they believe does not satisfy them.

So if Susan had known choice theory, as much as she wanted Dave to change, she would have known that all she could do was change the way *she* was choosing to live her life. If what she then chose to do became more satisfying to Dave than what she had been doing, it is likely he would have become more loving. If what she did was satisfying to her but Dave remained withdrawn, she might have come to the conclusion that she did not need him and file for divorce. But whatever she decided, she would have been aware that her efforts were directed at choosing to control herself, not Dave or anyone else.

As soon as she realized that misery was a bad choice, she would also have become aware that better choices are almost always available. This realization is always encouraging, but before she tried to find a better behavior, she would first have taken a look at the marriage pictures in her head. Mostly she would have found pictures in which Dave was acting much better than he had been recently—perhaps treating her with more kindness and spending more time with her doing things they both enjoyed. Because those were the pictures she wanted, she had been spending all her energy depressing and criticizing in an effort to get Dave to be more like these ideal pictures, but it had not paid off. As she looked at him, she would have realized he was far from the husband in her head.

To begin to take charge, she would stop focusing on these pictures that she couldn't achieve and try to find a few satisfying pictures in which she was doing something with Dave the way he was now. At any point, even in an unhappy marriage, there are almost always a few satisfying activities that the husband and wife still share. What Susan needed to do was to search her quality world for those still-satisfying marriage pictures, which likely still existed. For example, as difficult as things had gotten between them over the past several years, when she made the effort to plan a simple social evening at home with a few close friends, it was usually a success. As tense as things had become, if she stopped criticizing and complaining for a few days before the party, they almost always enjoyed a fun-filled and relaxing time.

For the past six months, however, she had paid little attention to this picture. If it crossed her mind that maybe a party would be fun, she had always been ready with excuses: she was too depressed, Dave never helped, the whole burden was on her, the people she invited always had a good time but never reciprocated. She'd had no difficulty finding many valid reasons for paying no attention to one of the most need-satisfying and achievable marriage pictures still remaining in her head. In the past, even when there had been tension between her and Dave for weeks, at the end of one of those relaxed social evenings Dave had been loving and attentive. She knew this, but like most people with marriage difficulties who don't know choice theory, she preferred to criticize and depress rather than plan such an evening.

The important lesson to be learned here is that when you are having difficulty getting along with someone important to you, you should spend your energy on pictures that you are fairly certain you can achieve. Susan should especially have looked for old ones that used to be fun: for example, the send-him-a-funny-greeting-card picture—he used to enjoy those cards so much. These pictures seemed inconsequential now that she was choosing to be so miserable, but she should have looked for them, as they were still there. She could even have made the effort to try to figure out a few new ones that might have been satisfying even in these bad times. I know it is hard for anyone depressing strongly to do this, but it is a sensible thinking behavior over which Susan had control, and she could have chosen to try to do it. The more she reminded herself that she was choosing to depress, the more apparent it would have become that this was a better choice.

We must keep in mind that each of us has his or her own quality world. If we search through all their nooks and crannies, we find them filled with pictures that we pasted into them years ago and have not looked at for a long time. But if they are there, they are still need-satisfying. If they were not, they could not be there.

Susan, however, did not have to settle for the few pictures she had of a better life with Dave; she could have created some more. Rather than continue to depress over pictures she couldn't achieve, she could have tried to tap her creativity to see if she could figure out some new situations that might be highly satisfying to both her and Dave. She can be compared to a driver vainly spinning her car wheels in the sand; she has to stop spinning her wheels, get out, and look for another way to get going.

You can't stop wanting any picture in your head, but you can select from your pictures those that you have a good chance of satisfying. Susan needed to avoid the common trap of saying, "If I can't have this specific picture, I don't want any." To get her marriage going again, a less satisfying picture would have been better than one she couldn't achieve. She could have told herself that she had the ability to put a lot of satisfying marriage pictures in her quality world. Some of them she might not achieve in the foreseeable future—maybe never. There would be some, however, that, no matter how bad her marriage had become, she still had the power to achieve. She could have said to herself, "As I do this, I will feel good, Dave will feel good, and our marriage will be better."

If Susan had known choice theory, she would not have stubbornly held out for six months for pictures she could not satisfy. As soon as she was dissatisfied, she would, for example, have planned a good social evening and carried out the plan. If it didn't work, she would have been out a little time and energy; but if it did, she would have made a small beginning toward regaining control of her marriage. At the end of that evening, it is likely that she would have found Dave attentive and in a good frame of mind. She could have mentioned how much she enjoyed doing this again and asked him if he could think of something else they might do together soon that he would enjoy. If he mentioned something, she would not have been vague and said something like, "That would be nice," or even, "We haven't done that for a while." If what he suggested was in any way acceptable to her (which at that close moment would be very likely), what she would have said was, "Fine, let's do it," and right then discuss when, where, and how she could help make it happen.

Besides the unplanned love and affection that continually occur in any good marriage, there are the tangible shared (and unshared) experiences that must be planned on a regular basis or the relationship will deteriorate. Even in the best marriages, these events must be planned; they will not spring forth on their own. The time to plan how and when to satisfy these important pictures is not when there is anger or tension but when there is love and closeness. As in this example, a good time is when the more dissatisfied partner has done something to recapture a little of the love and closeness that has long been absent from the relationship. In this marriage, there had not been a well-planned, tangibly satisfying event for six months, and it was during this time that Dave found another woman to provide some of what was missing. In fact, one of the excuses that he gave himself to stop guilting was that Susan was no fun anymore.

It is important that the reader understand that I don't believe that one or two fun parties can save a failing marriage—much more has to be done. I use this only as an example of one of many satisfying activities that one or both partners can attempt that will renew a dragging relationship. If they continue to spend their time and energy spinning old wheels that have long been stuck in the sand, they will accomplish nothing.

At this point I am sure some women reading this choice theory advice would say that everything I have suggested is only the woman's responsibility. Doesn't the man have any obligation to do something to correct the situation? Why should the whole burden be on the woman? The problem with this fair thinking is that it is an attempt to shift part of the burden to Dave, but we don't know whether or not he was as dissatisfied in the beginning, when the marriage might have been saved, as Susan was. If he was, of course, it was his responsibility. Certainly he should do all he can to make the marriage better, but he will do only what is satisfying to him. And if he was not dissatisfied and chose to do nothing but withdraw into his shell while Susan criticized and depressed, that was his choice.

Choice theory makes it clear that there is no way that Susan or anyone could have *forced* him to make another choice. He may eventually make a better choice, but this will be when he wants to, not when she asks him or forces him by her choice of misery. Arguing that it isn't fair or that "I won't unless he does" is logical, but it puts the shoe on a foot that Susan can't control. Fair or not, all Susan (or any of us) can do is control her own life. If she does it in a way that Dave also enjoys, he may decide to take a little more initiative in doing some things that are satisfying to her.

The other valid choice for Susan would have been to decide that if she had to take the initiative, she did not want the marriage. She could have made this clear to Dave, told him what she would and wouldn't do, and then ended the marriage if he did not do what she wanted. The problem with this direct, confrontational approach is that Dave might have said, "Let's end it." Even if he still wanted the marriage, he might have interpreted this direct approach as too controlling. If Susan had wanted to end her marriage, taking a direct, controlling approach would have been almost the sure way to do it. Most men and women who take this approach, however, are bluffing. If it does not work, they are not prepared to end their marriages. What they are well prepared to do is depress, headache, or get sick rather than look for and take the initiative to put into practice some mutually satisfying pictures that remain in both partners' heads.

Keep in mind that Susan was still trying to control Dave (and herself) with her misery. Of course, she had no idea that her misery was a chosen behavior or that it was the most satisfying choice for her at the time. But had she known choice theory and been willing to accept that she was choosing her miserable behavior, she still would have found it difficult to accept that when she chose a self-denying or altruistic behavior it was more for herself than anyone else. No matter how much she put herself out for Dave, her behavior was always for her benefit. The chances we take whenever we do something for another person are that someone else benefits a great deal, that someone else does little or no work—we do it all, or possibly that someone else is not appreciative or refuses to reciprocate. Susan had every right to hope or expect that Dave would be appreciative and helpful, *but she had no control over what he chose to do.*

For example, if Dave had become drunk and abusive when Susan planned a pleasant social evening, this would have been his choice. An evening that started with the best intentions would have ended disastrously. If this happened more than once, Susan would take these evenings out of her quality world. But until the party, she would have no way of knowing. Remember, she can only control her own life. Her happiness depends not on what others do but on what she does, and the sooner she learns this, the happier she will be.

If we had asked Susan, or even if Susan had asked herself, "What do you want?" the answer very likely would have been, "I don't know." This, of course, is impossible. As much as we may try to deny it, we always know what is in our quality worlds. If, however, we become discouraged because we can't get what we want, we lose control by convincing ourselves we don't know. As her marriage began to fail, Susan knew very well that what she wanted was a better marriage. Perhaps a long vacation with Dave would have given their marriage a needed boost, but it was easier to say "I don't know" than to face what seemed so remote at the time. To take charge of our lives, we must muster the strength to come to grips with what it is we want. This is because, although with effort we may block any frustration from awareness for a while,

---

We cannot stop ourselves from behavior until we are fully aware of what is frustrating us.

In an effort to deny what they really want, people like Susan often sigh and say, "What does it matter what I want? I'll never get it." But her sighs and depressing are still her way of choosing to suffer to try to get what she denies she wants. From the standpoint of the pain she chooses, it makes no difference if she is aware of what she wants or not. If we don't have what we want, we will choose to anger or suffer just the same. Once you know choice theory, you will not waste your time and energy refusing to face what you want just because it is hard to get, because you know that you will choose to suffer just the same.

To help us gain the courage to face what we want, we must keep in mind that, except for breathing, we almost always have more than one picture in our heads to satisfy any need. And if we don't have enough, we can add more. So rather than depress because Dave wouldn't take her on a trip, Susan should have looked for a picture that is close to what she wants that is possible for her to get. For example, there is no good reason that she could not have taken the trip without him. As soon as she got this idea, she could have come to grips with the fact that Dave was not an indispensable traveling companion. She could have gone with a friend and had a good time. Getting away from Dave would have given both a well-needed rest from each other.

As Susan learns choice theory, she will still continue to depress and choose other misery, but she will not choose these for as long as she has in the past. Knowing choice theory does not provide instant control, but because you are aware that you are choosing your misery, you will find it almost impossible to choose it for months or years as many people do. I often choose to be miserable for an hour or two, sometimes for as long as a day, but then I say to myself, "There must be a better choice." What I keep in mind, however, is that the better choice is always a doing behavior. As I've explained, we can directly and arbitrarily control only what we do. For example, Susan can host a social evening, but she cannot choose to feel better because she does. However, if the evening is a success, and if most of her evenings have been, she will likely choose to enjoy herself. There is nothing about a successful activity that will induce us to continue to choose misery.

Susan might also have to learn that she has to take some previously important pictures out of her quality world if she wishes to stay married to Dave. The main picture that most long-married people have to remove is the picture of the couple doing everything together. Getting married does not suddenly make all the pictures in the quality worlds of the couple correspond. We marry wisely when we and our spouses share a great many pictures, but as a marriage matures, there are bound to be important pictures that are not shared and must be satisfied separately or the marriage will suffer.

As we have already learned, Dave likes to ski more than Susan does. But she could have used this knowledge to the advantage of their marriage rather than to its detriment as she tended to do. She could, for example, have watched the snow reports, and as soon as there was snow, she could have taken the initiative and told Dave, "Don't miss the first snow—go skiing." She could have told him that she would be fine by herself, as there were some other things she would like to do. "Let's plan it right now." If Dave had any feeling for her at all, he would have made an effort to do more things with her when they were home together, because he would have known that she was not out to deprive him of what he enjoyed doing alone.

I can think of quite a few pictures my wife and I share and some that we don't. If we make sure to share on a regular basis and to encourage each other to enjoy what we don't share, we have the basis for a solid marriage. Even if we can't encourage each other to do what we don't share, the least we can do is to be tolerant of the fact that we are different people with different backgrounds. If we take this sensible approach and do not try to control each other into constant togetherness, we will usually be willing to share activities. Most people with successful marriages will do a reasonable amount just because the person they love wants to. If they don't encourage or at least tolerate what they don't share, they anger and become less tolerant.

If we have differences in marriage or any other relationship, the only way we can work them out is to negotiate a satisfactory compromise. Even a compromise is usually better for one party than the other, but if we compromise often enough, the advantages tend to even out. This is why we negotiate before we compromise—to make sure we get our fair share. It is sad to hear intelligent people who are suffering from differences between them say that there is no sense talking. Talking—or, more accurately, negotiating—is all we have to work out our differences. People too often choose to suffer, complain, criticize, fight, get sick, act crazy, or use drugs in an attempt to control someone else (or themselves) rather than working out their differences through negotiation.

If you are in any personal difficulty, it is almost always because you have not been able to figure out a way to negotiate differences with someone important to you in fulfilling your needs. It is the only way we have; if we can't avail ourselves of it, there are no alternatives. When people deride counseling as ineffective, what they are saying is that they do not want to negotiate—they want to control. As I explained before, when you attempt to use power, you almost always lose belonging, so we all must be willing to sacrifice a little power to satisfy other needs. How we do it and how much we do it is what negotiation is all about. The reason Susan should have looked for some pictures in their quality worlds that she and Dave could still share—and found the social evening—is that this sharing may have made it possible to negotiate and reach other compromises that may have saved the marriage. We can live with differences; no marriage is without them. But if we refuse to negotiate when these differences become extreme, we lose any chance to salvage the marriage.

Do the Susans and Daves of the world need professional counseling when they lose control of their marriage or any other part of their lives? The answer is clear: if they try to work it out on their own and can't, they should see a good counselor. But a good counselor is not one who accepts that their misery happens to them or that simply talking about misery, past or present, will help them to make better choices. Good counseling focuses on what they are choosing to do now. Is it getting them what they want? Since it never is (or they wouldn't be there), a good counselor negotiates a plan with one or both of them to do something better. The plan is always a way for them to satisfy important pictures in their heads within their marriage. The plan may also be to find new pictures that are mutually satisfying if what they have seems insufficient.

Good counseling does not poke excessively into the past, and when the past is discussed, it is always related to the present. If people have had traumatic pasts, they should be able to share them with the counselor so that she has some idea of when their lives went out of control. But it is the counselor's job to help whoever comes—Susan, Dave, or both—to understand that, as bad as things were, what went on then may have little or no bearing on what is going on now.

The greatest value of discussing the past is not for its misery but for the strengths it may provide that can be used now. In a sense, Susan was looking into her past when she searched her quality world for marriage pictures that once worked well for both her and Dave. There is no sense looking for something new if something old that was satisfying can be used again. Many people, however, try to avoid a difficult present by believing that the terrible things that happened to them are still overwhelming and that unless these past events can be brought to a satisfactory resolution, they will not get well.

Susan may claim that her problems with Dave are just like the problems she had with her father. She may have had serious problems with her father, but to blame her marriage difficulties on that is a fallacy. She is not married to her father, and if she depresses with Dave as she did with him, she is choosing the same ineffective behavior now as she did then. Once she knows choice theory (which counselors who use it also teach to their clients), she will quickly learn that just because she made a bad choice then, she does not have to continue making it now. As she begins to make better choices now, her life with her father will soon be forgotten. We live now and must satisfy ourselves now. We can't go back into our pasts actually or verbally and satisfy conditions that no longer exist.

It is unfortunate that many professional counselors who do not know choice theory encourage clients to live in the past rather than teaching them what they need to know to deal with the present. Clients should be wary of counselors who support them in their efforts to control important people in their present lives by attempting to impress them with how much they suffered in the past. Dave could easily get turned off to Susan if, supported by what she had learned in counseling, she continually confronted him with how much he was like her father and how difficult this was for her. If her father is dead, this would put Dave in a totally out-of-control, no-win position that would persuade him more to withdraw than to attempt to work out their differences.

Miserable things have happened to us all. Many people have been through the tortures of concentration camps and gone ahead and lived their lives. They have figured out that they must satisfy their needs now without attempting to do so by controlling others with what they have suffered and continue to choose to suffer. The only satisfaction we can get with and from others is what they choose to give us. Any time we try to force them to give us what we want by attempting to control them with suffering, past or present, we will fail. If, as we often do when we fail, we choose additional suffering, we engage in a futile, losing effort. Keep in mind that to satisfy the pictures in our heads, we will choose to suffer pain beyond belief. If, however, we learn that our misery is a choice and that better choices are almost always available, we will make an active effort, by ourselves or with help, to choose more effective behaviors.

When we learn choice theory, we must be humble enough to accept the fact that, try as we will (and suffer as we will), there is no way we can actually control even a small portion of the world around us. There are many times when no matter what we do, think, or feel, we cannot satisfy ourselves the way we would like. But the fact is we can't have control over what others do and think. If we can figure out something that will satisfy us even a little, we are infinitely better off than if we had wasted our time choosing misery in an effort to control situations outside ourselves and what we do.

As we regain some small degree of control, we gain confidence that we can gain more. If Susan figures out what she can do that she and Dave will enjoy and then goes ahead and does it, she will gain some control over a situation that before was out of control. If Dave also enjoys it and moves closer to her, she can begin the delicate process of negotiating some of the pictures that they do not share. If, together, they can work out some compromises and put them into practice, she will stop choosing misery, and he will stop withdrawing. If she does these things without thinking of what's fair but because they are the only sensible things she can do for the marriage, and if Dave cares for her at all, they will recoup their marriage. If she does all this and he still does not want to be married to her, then she has done all she can and should look elsewhere for love.

14. Choice Theory Psychology and Raising Children

We may not all agree on exactly what a well-raised child is, but most of us share some general pictures in our heads of what we would like to see our children become. We want them to be warm and loving; hardworking and financially prudent; careful about their health (we especially don't want them to use drugs); moral and law-abiding; and both caring and respectful of their friends, family, and family friends. If this were the way my children turned out, I would consider that anything I had done to help them become this way was effective parenting.

I would like to explain some choice theory basics of child-rearing to parents whose children still live with them that may help them avoid mistakes. This chapter is not intended to be a complete guide to raising children, but assuming that the reader is now familiar with choice theory, it should prove useful to any parent.

One of the most important choice theory lessons we can learn is that we should try to keep the pictures of what we want our children to become as general as those described above. As soon as we try to push our children to become the specific people that they may be in our heads, we become less effective as parents. For example, the more we want them to be doctors, lawyers, engineers, army officers, ministers, married, parents, rich, famous, or any other specific picture in our heads, the more we will push them to achieve these goals *for us*. And unfortunately, nothing that we do will alienate a child more than pushing him or her to be something he or she does not want to be.

To satisfy their needs, children want to pursue their own goals. If this were not the case, we would still be in caves, mindlessly doing exactly as our parents wished. Progress has been made because children are willing to struggle for what satisfies them regardless of their parents. Too many parents attempt to mold their children to the parents' pictures, and for them, parenting turns into a losing power struggle. Love and caring are swept aside as the parent-child relationship degenerates into angering and criticizing.

Many parents, especially those with definite pictures of what their children should become as adults, may balk at our suggestion to let children figure out the specific ways they want to live their lives. They may argue, "If I don't show him the way, he will amount to nothing. How can I stand by and take a chance with my child's life?" There is much that a good parent can do to help a child succeed in the general way I described in the first paragraph of this chapter. Parents who consider this general description of a successful child insufficient and insist that their children's success is dependent upon their becoming exactly what the parents want will be more of a hindrance than a help.

Ask yourself, "Am I living the life I want to live, or is it the life my parents picked out for me?" My guess is that it's much more yours than theirs, and I also guess that what you are now doing is satisfying. But if it isn't, I still do not believe that you are spending much time regretting that you did not follow your parents' guidance. I also guess that even if the life you chose is working out well, your parents hindered you along the way and did not accept that your choice was sensible until it became apparent to everyone that it was.

The only specific picture that my wife and I adhere to strongly with our grown children is that we like them to be at our house on some of the holidays and, while there, to make an effort to get along well with each other. We also have the picture that they be on good terms with us and with each other. Past that, as much as we can, we try to keep in our heads the general picture of them doing with their lives what they think is best and succeeding. With the help of choice theory, we have finally begun to appreciate that they are going to live according to their pictures, not ours. But whatever we can do to persuade them to keep a picture in their heads of staying on good terms with us and with each other, we will try to do.

How responsible are we for the way our children turn out? For example, is it mostly our fault if a child chooses to behave in an aberrant manner like Tim, the pot-smoking nonstudent of chapter 3? We certainly have the responsibility to make an effort to learn what to do that will make it less likely that any child of ours will turn out to be like Tim at sixteen. Most children give consideration to what their parents want, but if they do not agree, they, like Tim, will do what they think is best. What we can do is raise them in a way that makes it less likely that they will be irresponsible, unhappy adults. Tim's parents do not realize that much of his present self-destructive behavior is his way of resisting their pressure that he start now to prepare to become a lawyer by doing well in school. His way of resisting is detrimental to him, but there is no doubt that it has worked. They no longer aspire for him to be a lawyer. They would be satisfied now if he would just pass in school, stop smoking pot, and turn off his music on school nights at a decent hour.

In chapter 3, I suggested that Tim's father make an effort to rebuild his rapidly deteriorating relationship with Tim, because if he doesn't, there will be little he can do to help Tim change. Without a good relationship, our effect upon one another is either nonexistent or destructive. Nowhere is this more important than when you raise a child, so it is fundamental to all child-raising that you try to keep yourself as a loving person in your child's head. This is never easy to do, especially if you follow the commonsense fallacy that if your child is misbehaving, all you have to do is show more concern, stop being permissive, and make him or her behave. The more you try to make the child behave, the more he or she resists, and very soon the two of you are hardly on speaking terms. All of us know parents who are neither unconcerned nor permissive yet whose children are behaving like Tim or worse, and they can't make them change even with punishment and threats. What these parents have to learn is patience. It is a slow, difficult task to rebuild the tenuous relationship that always exists between a parent and a resistant child like Tim, but unless this relationship is improved, nothing we do will work.

Part of the way Tim resists the continuing pressure from his parents is to begin to remove them from his quality world as need-satisfying people. As he does, he will pay little attention to what they want and even less to what they do. In this situation most parents tend to make the mistake of pushing harder, with the unfortunate result that a child like Tim takes them more and more out of his head. If, at the end of this vicious cycle, Tim has taken his parents completely out of his head—as many like Tim do—his parents pay attention to the conflict rather than to what Tim really needs, which is a good relationship with them. Even if his parents finally learn a better way to deal with him, it may be too late, because he will have replaced them with other pictures; now he is attempting to satisfy his need to belong with drugs and other harmful behaviors. That is why in chapter 3 I suggested that Tim's father invite him to go fishing—this is a picture they still share in their quality worlds. If the trip is successful and Tim begins to put his father back into his head as a need-satisfying person, then the necessary ground has been prepared to go further.

If, after a few fishing trips, the relationship with his father becomes more secure, they may eventually settle on the plan that if Tim does better in school, he may use the family car. This or any other plan must be worked out in a way that does not frustrate Tim severely if he does not follow through. Frustration can be a valuable learning experience for Tim (or anyone) if he can learn to deal with it effectively, but Tim has a long way to go before he can handle much frustration. If, after a few weeks, Tim is no longer carrying out the plan and slacks off in school, his father should take the car away—but when he does, he should make sure that Tim knows exactly what he can do to get it back. Tim does not have a great many patient behaviors, so if the car is taken away for too long, he will look at it as forever and may quickly revert to his old ways, reject his parents, and then they are back to square one. The plan must make it possible for him to get the car back in a reasonable time, such as two weeks. This will seem hard but still possible, and he will keep his father in his head as a fair person whom he needs and with whom he will continue to plan.

In general, what I am going to suggest in the rest of this chapter about raising children assumes that the parent continues to make an effort to maintain a good relationship. While these suggestions apply to children of all ages including Tim at sixteen, they are directed more to small children. If Tim's parents had used the choice theory that is suggested in this chapter from the beginning, they might have prevented the problems they are now having with him.

Before twelve or thirteen years of age, most children are fairly easy to get along with. If not, at least the parents still see them as small and don't worry that their disobedience is going to ruin their lives. They may not obey us as much as we'd like, or perhaps they are mean to sisters or brothers, but in important matters like avoiding danger, protecting their health, and going to school, they still listen to us, because they have a powerful need to belong, and we are the ones they most count upon to satisfy this need. But children, even quite disobedient ones, tend to take their parents for granted. They sense how much we love them and they believe (correctly) that we will put up with a lot of bad treatment from them and still continue to stand by them if they need our help. I can't explain why we have such strong love for our children, but we do—they know it, and they will take advantage of it to control us if we let them. But we cannot be effective parents if they control us any more than they can be effective children if we are too much in control of them.

It is during this time, the thirteen-year grace period, that we must learn how to deal with them effectively, and the earlier we start applying the principles of choice theory, the easier the process of child-raising should be. If they stop loving us—and eventually they might if we try too hard to control them—persuading them to change if they are self-destructive becomes much more difficult. Even after all the hostility between Tim and his father, they still had some love for each other, so the situation was hopeful.

The main problem that confronts parents in raising children is how they can live amicably with each other and still satisfy their own pictures. When there are differences, as there almost always are—for example, when we want them to do homework and they want to watch television—the parents are almost always much more dissatisfied than the children, so it is more up to us than our children to figure out a way to resolve these differences. But driven by our need for power, we rarely think of resolving differences with our children—we want to control them. After all, isn't it natural for us to control our children for their own good? Nothing in this chapter suggests that we not intervene in our children's lives—that we leave them alone to do as they wish. We should not abdicate our role as parents, and few children, short of maturity, would want us to. Children welcome parental control if they love their parents, but they don't want to be totally controlled. At almost any age, they want parents to grant them the power to do what they consider reasonable with their lives.

The question is not whether to control but rather what is reasonable and how much control a parent should try to exert. The answer to this question depends a lot on what the child wants. If you believe what he or she wants is irresponsible, you need to exert more control than if his or her wants are more acceptable. A child who wants to travel around the city by hitchhiking instead of riding a bike or taking a bus is a child who needs direction. This is why it is so important to have a good relationship with your children: so that they will both tell you what they want and accept some control from you if what they want is, in your judgment, irresponsible. If, at any age, what a child wants is far from what you want but you have a good relationship, you can usually negotiate the differences and work out a compromise you can both accept. In Tim's case the trouble was that before he and his father went fishing, the relationship had deteriorated to the point where negotiation and compromise were no longer possible.

Because all of us, young and old, have such a strong need for power, negotiation and compromise are the only ways that both parent and child can fulfill this need and still get along with each other. Almost all the difficulties we run into as we raise children are due to our failure to understand that these are the only effective behaviors we have when children do not do as we like (or we do not do as they like). Parents who do not negotiate but try to force their children to fulfill the parents' pictures regardless of what the children may want always find themselves angering or bribing to try to gain some control. Children who love you will almost always compromise and accept reasonable control if you take the time to negotiate differences: explain why you want what you want and listen to their reasons for what they want. But they will resist bitterly any authority figure not willing to negotiate or compromise.

Like all of us, they will try to satisfy their own pictures, and if they have to fight parents who won't compromise, they will do that too. As I have explained, this fighting may take the form of direct angering, but since children, compared to parents, have little actual power, their fighting usually takes a more indirect form, such as withdrawal, depressing, disobedience, psychosomatic illness, or drug use. What Tim chose to do to satisfy himself is typical of children whose parents have spent little time trying to find out what their children want and negotiating differences when they arise.

Although successful parenting is a complex task, some of the complexity can be removed by reducing how we deal with children to one basic axiom:

Try as hard as possible to teach, show, and help your children to gain effective control of their own lives.

This means that, as much as you can, you should never do anything to or for a child that will cause the child to believe he or she has lost control. All the irresponsible behaviors children choose when growing up are their attempts to take control of their lives. If they blame their parents for any undesirable outcomes of their choices—as, right or wrong, they frequently do—the relationship between them and their parents suffers. The blaming, in turn, causes even more loss of control. When Tim did not succeed in school, he lost control. When his parents pushed, he blamed them for his problems and refused to accept his own inadequacy. When he took to smoking pot and withdrawing into his room to listen to music, this was his self-destructive way to regain control. His parents might have been more effective if they had kept in mind that their role from the time their children were born was to help them to gain and maintain effective control of their lives. His parents did not realize that they had failed to teach Tim to be responsible. Until he took over his life at age sixteen, Tim was never taught how to take charge of his life.

To help our children gain control of their lives, we should be aware that as we raise them, all of us employ four separate and easily understood procedures. Everything we do with our children, simple or complex, can be related to one of these clear-cut procedures. Once you learn them, which you should find very easy to do, you will mostly use the ones that are effective and reduce to a minimum the procedures you use that are ineffective. These four procedures are as follows:

- **Do things for them.** For example, we feed them when they are young or take them into our businesses when they are grown.

- **Do things to them.** For example, if they don't do as we want, we punish them when they are little or disown them when they are grown.

- **Do things with them.** For example, we play with them when they are small and discuss mutual interests like sports and music with them when they are grown.

- **Leave them be.** For example, we let them cry out a temper tantrum when they are two years old or say nothing but wish them well and make plans to keep in close touch when, at age eighteen, they tell us that they are going to strike out on their own.

I believe very strongly that many of us tend to do too much *for* our children if what we want is for our children to be in control of their lives when they are grown. This is especially true when they are small: we carry them and dress them when they could walk or dress themselves. We do it because we love them and because it is easier and quicker to do it for them than to wait while they do it themselves. But another reason we do many things for our children is to control them. We hope that they will appreciate what we do and pay attention to what we want as they grow. We also do far too much *to* them, as when we yell at them and punish them when they do not do what we want.

We do not do enough purely *with* our children without concurrently doing *for* them or *to* them. For example, we go for a walk with a young child because we both want to go, but when she gets tired and complains, we carry her home. Then, because we are tired from carrying her, we may yell at her because of what we decided to do (carry her) when she complained of being too tired to walk. What started out as a good do-with-her experience deteriorated into a do-for-her-and-to-her experience—which did not help her to be in control of her life. If we had been more patient, taken a rest, and insisted that she walk home even if she walked slowly, we would not have yelled at her. We also should have been smart enough not to walk so far that she was likely to lose control by getting too tired.

Children need us. They need our company, instruction, love, and support. They need to know where we are and that they can count on us for help and guidance. But they do not need us all the time. At all ages, we don't leave children alone enough. For example, on a rainy day, when they are perfectly capable of figuring out how to entertain themselves, as soon as they complain, we start doing *for* them and *to* them. Too often, we start to play with them, get bored, quit, and then ask them to leave us alone. We would be better off letting them alone in the first place to figure out what to do on their own. In many situations, instead of letting them get up their own games, we get far too involved. Activities like Little League, where adults' needs are being satisfied as much or more than children's, teach children to rely on others, not themselves, and that they have little or no power even in play. Play then becomes frustrating and fails to be the good learning experience that it should be. What they learn is that adults make all the key decisions, which causes them to lose control, not gain it, and when they get older and have to make decisions, they don't know how.

When Tim was small, he was a good boy; the present trouble did not start until he was fourteen years old. What probably contributed to the way he is behaving now is that when he was small his parents did far too much *for* him and *to* him. They imposed a lot of their thinking on him, and because it was easy and mostly satisfying, he did what he was told and followed the rules. Even though it was not always satisfying, he did this because his parents did do a lot *for* him. If he got behind in his easy elementary-school work, his parents pitched in and helped him. If he wanted a fancy bicycle that cost a lot of money, they bought it for this good boy. He continued to be good, but because too much was done for him and to him, he was not in control of his life; his parents were.

Because too much had been done for him earlier, when he got to high school, he was unprepared for the many mature things that he now had to do for himself. Without confidence and lacking good preparation, he began doing little in school, and to get him to do more, his concerned parents tried to force him to work harder. Now they stopped doing *for* him and began to do a lot *to* him. They yelled, threatened, and restricted in an attempt to control him as they had done easily when he was small by doing things *for* him. But they were powerless to help him to satisfy the strong social and sexual needs that were churning inside of him; all their doing *to* him accomplished was that he chose to withdraw and began to take them out of his quality world. We keep no pictures in our heads of people who do things *to* us.

When he found himself failing because he could not handle the academic demands of high school, he no longer even pretended to make an effort. His parents cut off his allowance, and he lost the little control that money could buy. Now, to regain control of his life, Tim rationalized that the hard work his parents were demanding of him was more for them than for him. He stated very strongly that he did not need algebra or college-prep English, that the teachers had it in for him, that everybody smoked pot, and that his music and his friends (young people like himself) were all he cared about. What he was doing was regaining control over his life with the meager behaviors he had. When his parents started to apply heavy pressure, it was like beating a badly lame horse, and the impasse was reached after about a year and a half of high school.

To avoid these common problems, from the time their children are small, parents should teach them how to take control of their own lives. To do this, they should avoid doing what Tim's parents did, which was too much *for* him and *to* him, in a mistaken effort to get him to do what they thought was right. Even with infants, we should concentrate on doing nothing for them that they can do for themselves and as much with them as we can without being overwhelming or intrusive. We should also leave them alone to deal with the world on their own for short but increasing periods of time starting when they are in their cribs.

For example, when a little baby is fed, loved, cleaned, and played with and then gets cranky, it may be best to leave him alone. Even at several months, he may be checking out his power to control his parents. If he takes control through crying or fussing, he will quickly learn that when he is uncomfortable, he can cry, gain control through misery, and get his parents to do *for* him. He fails to learn to do for himself. When you leave a well-cared-for infant alone when he is obviously tired and you can no longer do anything helpful for him (you can't sleep for him), you are being loving, not cruel. When he discovers he is on his own, he will cry mightily for quite a while, but very quickly he will learn to settle down and amuse himself with tiny thoughts or a crib toy or go to sleep with no hard feelings toward you at all. Even in infancy there are easily learned options that can be used to replace the angering with which we are born.

When Tim was small, he was urged to do what his parents wanted him to do: go to bed, get up, and play with these (not those) children. He did not, however, suffer from overwhelming control. In fact, he went along easily because his parents were warm and loving, but the result was that he was mostly involved in activities that his parents selected for him. They were never cruel, and most of what they wanted for him he found sensible and fun to do, so it was easy for him to cooperate. But even at five and six, he should have been learning not only to cooperate but also to *operate*—to make some decisions and to carry them out.

For example, when he was six, he didn't like to come in for lunch during the summer when he was outside playing. He would show up starving at about three, and his mother would make him a big lunch, but then he was so full that he had trouble eating his dinner. No parent should force a child to eat, and if he didn't want to come for lunch when his mother fed his sister and herself, she should have told him to work out lunch on his own. She should have shown him where the food was and pointed out that if he fed himself, he also had to clean up. He could then have decided what to do, but whatever it was, it would have been his decision and he would have been left alone to make it. If he didn't eat lunch some days, his parents should not have worried. There is no danger that boys like Tim will become malnourished if they skip an occasional meal.

When Tim was ten, he wanted an expensive iPod. Instead of buying it for him, his parents should have negotiated with him to do some work around the house to help pay for it. They also should have discussed how long he could play it, what time he had to turn it off for the night, and how early he could turn it on in the morning.

I don't believe that I need write more examples of how it is better to do less *for* or *to* your children. You can figure this out on your own with your child if you accept that effective behaviors are not learned unless we do things for ourselves or with someone who will show and share but not take over or impose his or her will upon us. We learn responsibility only by taking it, and children need to follow through to help get what they say they want. If they get in trouble, they should be allowed to suffer reasonable and natural consequences before an adult steps in. If they get in way over their heads, we should help them to help themselves as much as we can, but we should do as little directly for them as makes sense in the situation.

Suppose your twelve-year-old promises several neighbors that she will help out by minding their young children for about three hours a day, and they count on her to do this. Then a girlfriend's family suddenly invites her to go camping for two weeks, and she asks if she can go. You ask her about the child care, and she begs you to go to the neighbors and get her off the hook. She is a good girl and you are tempted to do this or find someone to take her place, because this has come up rather suddenly. What you should do is let her handle it. If she does it badly by just going off, you should talk to the neighbors and ask them to talk to her about it when she returns. Ask them to do this as a favor to you. If they complain to you that you should not have let her go, tell them that the contract was with her, not you. This is a rough learning experience, and no matter how she handles it, she will learn the most if she does it herself.

What makes children strong and capable as well as warm and loving is a lot of parental involvement—a lot of the with-them procedure. We cannot hug, kiss, and talk with them enough. We should also involve ourselves in playing with them, teaching them, and especially helping them to carry out responsible plans successfully even when they do not coincide with ours. When she was sixteen, our daughter, who had been corresponding with a Japanese pen pal for about two years, told us that he had invited her to come to Japan and that she wanted to go. This was not the picture in our heads, but we told her that if she could work out all the details and the complicated protocol, we would help pay for the trip. We would advise her, but she had to do everything to get ready on her own. She did, and taking control of a complex situation and carrying it out well was a wonderful learning experience for her.

To satisfy the strong need to belong, children should be encouraged to find friends (on their own) to play with. Finding friends at five (assuming other children are available) is good practice for the more complex teenage social scene later. When they do find friends, we should be careful to be accepting of the children they find. If the friends they find are not the ones we'd like to see them with, we might talk to them, but we should not interfere too much, or they will lose control in a very delicate and important area. How to deal with friends is very difficult, if not impossible, to teach, but it is usually very easily learned if adults do not interfere.

It is also valuable to work with children on simple tasks where they can see that they are making a contribution to the family. This fulfills their need for power in a way that helps them to become effective. The assignment of helping with your younger brothers and sisters is especially valuable, as is yard work or even pitching in on a big project like painting the house. When we work with them, we must be patient and not rush to do things for them because they are slow. Instruct them and show them, but let them do their part of the task, and they will gain strength and confidence.

What makes children especially strong is for them to tackle a creative or competitive skill outside of school, one that requires work and discipline but is not adult-dominated like some highly organized children's athletics. Music, ballet, art, woodworking, car repair, swimming, model building, computer programming, and electronics are examples. The whole point of these is to help children experience the satisfaction that comes from a challenging, nonroutine activity to which they can contribute something creative of their own. The more they are able to do this on their own or with only occasional parental help but a lot of parental interest, the stronger they will be.

Nothing is more motivating than an activity in which we experience our inherent, always-present creativity. Hobbies or any *noncompetitive* activities, such as playing a musical instrument, are excellent motivators (if the child wants to play, not if she is forced), because the quiet time provided by many of these activities is when we experience creative moments. The more a child experiences her creativity, the more she will depend on it and learn to use it. In doing so, she will become familiar with one of the strongest forces we have for maintaining effective control of our lives. (This will be explained further in chapter 16 where I discuss creative, in-control time.) Tim dabbled, but he never followed through, and his greatest effort at present is obtaining marijuana.

What Tim lacked in his life was the confidence that comes only from accomplishment. He had never accomplished much more than being good when he was little, but being good got both him and his parents a lot of what they all wanted at the time. The trouble with being good is that it is too easy. There is no challenge, nothing creative—all you do is follow a few simple family rules, and you get taken care of. But as a child grows older, being good—which too often means that if you aren't, your parents will do things *to* you, and if you are, they will do things *for* you—doesn't work. This is because what you want at sixteen you can't get by people doing it *for* you or *to* you. You can't succeed in high school or as an adult just by being good. You have to work. You can't make friends with hardworking young people if they see you as lazy, so you turn to friends who, like yourself, do little that is constructive. To have fun, you depend less on active pursuits like team athletics or hobbies and more on the passive pleasures of drugs and music. This does not mean that young people who are active do not use drugs or listen to music, but they do not depend upon them, and that is a big difference.

In a sense, even though Tim was driving his parents crazy, he was still being good. He was hanging around the house doing nothing as he had done when he was little, but now, instead of this being good, it was no good. But we can't do more unless we know how and have a picture in our heads of satisfying accomplishment. If we have never worked on our own, there will be no picture. Now, as he is getting more involved with his mother and father, who have finally learned not to do things *to* him or *for* him but *with* him, Tim is starting at sixteen to try to learn what he should have learned at six. He can do it, but he is far behind. Some like Tim never catch up. They get married and then drink a lot of beer while their wives (this is typical of the wives of alcoholics) repeat the mistakes of the parents, doing a lot *to* them and *for* them but little or nothing *with* them.

Parents need to learn that children are born without knowing how to fulfill their needs. They must learn a lot or they will never take charge of their lives. They learn nothing by having things done to them and very little if things are done for them. They learn a lot from adults who do things with them and encourage them to do for themselves. It is not by chance that animals throw their young out on their own when their genetic instructions tell them they have done enough. An animal that cannot learn to fend for itself will not survive and therefore will leave no faulty descendants.

Unlike animals, we are too helpless to be thrown out when we are young; a great deal must be done for us or we won't survive. But as we mature, the care has to diminish, and doing *for* must move to doing *with* and then doing *alone.* Effective parents rejoice in the accomplishments their children achieve on their own; ineffective parents depress or anger when they find they have to do *for* adult children because they have not learned to do for themselves.

To raise effective children, we must try our best to take specific pictures of what they should become as adults out of our heads. We should keep in our heads mostly short-term pictures of our children behaving responsibly by working hard in school, helping around the house, caring for their possessions, being warm and friendly with peers who are friendly to them, and being able to be by themselves and figure out something to do that is satisfying and responsible. They should also be willing and able to talk with us when we have a difference of opinion and to negotiate a way that satisfies us both. If we have children who satisfy these general pictures, it is likely that whatever they decide to do with their lives will be acceptable to us or, if it isn't, that they will be willing to negotiate.

But even if we do all I suggest, there will be plenty of times as our children grow when they will break rules and then challenge us to do something about it. What we ordinarily do is called punishment or discipline, but choice theory explains that these are not the same. Self-discipline is effective; punishment is not—and the difference is clear. Self-discipline—the choice theory way—always starts with trying to teach children to follow reasonable rules through negotiation. Punishment—external control—starts and finishes with trying to force children to follow rules, even unreasonable rules, by inflicting pain if they refuse. (A reasonable rule is defined as one most children who are on good terms with their parents will follow with little protest; an unreasonable rule is one to which even usually obedient children strongly object.)

Punishment is inflicting pain, physical or mental, in the hope that the rule breaker will remember the pain and follow the rule next time. Once the pain is inflicted, the child has no way to avoid it—it is done. The punished child feels a deep loss of power and control, and he or she usually attempts to deal with this loss through choosing the painful and self-destructive feeling behavior of shaming. There is ordinarily no teaching or negotiating in the punishment way and no attempt to make sense of the rules a part of the procedure. If the punished child decides that the pain is worth whatever is gained by breaking the rule, then the punishment is ineffective. The most serious flaw in punishment is that it does not take into account the fact that the rule breaker is trying to satisfy a picture in his or her head. Unlike self-discipline, there is nothing in the punishment procedure to teach a child that there is likely another picture or a better choice of behavior that would be within the rules.

Punishment is by far the most widely used of all human control procedures, and the fact that so many punished children and adults continue to be out of control is sad testimony to the ineffectiveness of this traditional external-control procedure. Nowhere is this more apparent than in the failure of our overcrowded, punitive prisons, which release people who are less in control of their lives than when they went in. Probation, on the other hand, is a disciplinary procedure that is almost always effective if the probation officer is well-trained and not overloaded, as too many are now. In a society where choice theory was practiced, only the very dangerous (still unfortunately huge numbers) would be sent to prison; the rest would be treated with strict but creative probation, where they would learn choice theory to regain control of their lives.

What choice theory suggests is that we never punish any child. To deal with a very young child, under two and a half, who is too young to understand that she broke the rule, it is sensible to restrain her firmly, but not painfully, and tell her no in a stern voice when, for example, she turns on the gas or pinches her little brother. If the tiny child loves you, the restraint accompanied by a strong no is sufficient. When we deal with a child of three, old enough to know that she broke the rule, we should always use choice theory and never punish. A three-year-old who spills her milk both for attention and to be assertive can be told that she is responsible for cleaning up the mess. If it takes her a while and she is a little messy in doing it, it is still better than doing it for her or yelling at her. If she refuses, she should be told that she can go to her room until she decides to clean it up. She should also be served her milk in a wide glass, half-full, to prevent it from happening again due to clumsiness. But even if she spills her milk by accident, she, not her parent, should correct it.

Suppose your eight-year-old does not come home for dinner, and you have to scour the neighborhood to find her. She is well aware that she should have come home, so you talk to her to teach her what to do to prevent it from happening again. In this negotiation, she affirms that she respects the rule, and you work it out so that next time she will tell you where she is going. She also agrees that if she leaves that place for another child's house, she will call and let you know. You agree that if she is not home on time, you will call and tell her to come home.

This works for a while, but then she stops coming home, and when you call, she isn't where she said she would be. Basically, she found the plan too restrictive and, to assert her power, decided not to follow it.

Now you no longer talk but apply a sanction. You tell her that she has to stay home until she can make a plan to come home for dinner when she is playing at a friend's house. She doesn't want to stay home and she cries, but you are firm: she cannot go out after school the next day unless she has a plan. You offer to help her with the plan, but she has to have one. You do not hit her, threaten her, or yell at her, but you do insist that she stay home until she has a plan. With an eight-year-old, the plan can be as simple as just solemnly promising to come home on time from now on. It could also be that she will ask her older brother to remind her if he is near or that she will call home and ask if she may stay a little longer, but if she may not, she will come right home.

What the plan is with a young child is not important—what is important is that she have a plan that she can put into action. If she can do it, she has responsible control and learns the value of having it. If you punish by hitting or yelling in the hope that she will remember the pain and not do it again, she has no control. You can never take back a slap or a yell. It is done, she suffered it, and now she has even less control than she had previously. She will probably compound the problem by choosing to anger or depress in an attempt to regain control by controlling you that way.

Tim accepted the plan his father offered that when he started to do school work, he would gain the use of the car. It could have been a part of the disciplinary plan for his father to pay for a tutor to help him to learn to do the work, because if Tim could not do it without help, the plan would become punitive. If he began to do the work and then stopped after a few weeks, the car would again be taken away until he started studying. Tim fully accepted his commitment to this plan, and his parents did not allow him to pressure them into renegotiation.

The next time you are faced with a child old enough to negotiate with, try the following four steps. You will have a good chance to succeed not only in working out a solution to the problem but also in teaching your child to be more effective in the future.

1. Check the picture in your head of what you want from the child and make sure that what you want is also reasonably satisfying for the child. If the child is breaking the rule, be sure the rule is reasonable—which means it is one that most children would follow and one that you were willing to follow when you were a child. Work on your relationship with the child by doing something with him or her that you both enjoy and that has no direct bearing on the problem. (A good way to reach Tim might be to offer to listen to some of his music and let him explain it to you, but you should not try to get close by smoking or drinking with him.)

2. Try to wait until both you and the child have calmed down, and then, with as little angering as is possible for you in the situation, ask the child if he or she is satisfied with what he or she is doing or if he or she understands that it is against the rules.

3. When the child is not satisfied or admits to breaking a rule, negotiate a better way for the child to satisfy him- or herself and you. If you are involved in this plan, make sure that what you do is as much *with* and as little *to* or *for* the child as possible. It is better when the child can carry out the plan by him- or herself.

4. When the child claims to be satisfied with what he or she is doing and does not want to change, then, if you have the power, invoke a sanction that does not cause the child to lose control. The sanction is always some loss of freedom until the problem is worked out. Make sure that the child is able to change; if he or she needs help here, offer instruction or arrange for outside help, but don't do it for the child. Also make sure that the loss of freedom or privileges is not for long: ten minutes is the maximum for a five-year-old; an evening without television might be right for a ten-year-old. Whatever the action, it should be appropriate for the child's age and long enough for the child to see some sense in negotiating. It should not be so long that he or she gives up and does not want to try to correct the situation.

This advice can be extended to children of any age. I now associate mostly with people with grown children, and the greatest difficulty I see is that they still do too much to or for their children. They do these things partly because it is difficult for parents of grown children, whom they love, to bow gracefully out of their children's everyday lives. Since it becomes increasingly difficult to do things *with* them, the parents make the mistake of doing too much *for* them instead of just leaving them alone. If the children are ungrateful—as many are when they view what is done for them as an attempt to control them—they may withdraw and stay away. If they do, the parents may begin to do things *to* them, such as depressing in an attempt to control them by causing them to guilt.

To keep on good terms with adult children, continue to be warm and loving, but do as little as is possible *for* them or *to* them and as much *with* them as you both enjoy, and respect them enough to be willing to leave them *alone* if this is what they want.

When children reach the middle years, their forties to sixties, things between child and parent seem to reverse. Now, with equally unsatisfactory results, the child starts to do too much to and for the parent. In chapter 5, I mentioned Phyllis and her mother Carol as an example of this situation, and I will discuss them in much more detail in the next chapter.

15. Controlling Ourselves or Others with Pain or Misery

Most of us have people in our families very much like seventy-four-year-old, physically healthy Carol and her middle-aged daughter, Phyllis, whom I discussed in chapter 5. The mother, Carol, could be called a professional depresser. She attempted to control Phyllis with her endless complaints of misery. Phyllis had to be at her beck and call or Carol would withdraw into painful silence until Phyllis begged her to relent. Phyllis escaped from Carol's clutches through periodic migraining, and like many people we know, she would benefit from learning enough choice theory to deal with Carol and those like her more effectively. But perhaps Carol, who lives a life of excruciating, self-chosen suffering, would benefit as much or more than Phyllis from this knowledge. Carol will probably never learn choice theory as a theory, but if Phyllis can learn it and put it into practice with her, Carol, without realizing it, will learn enough to live a much more satisfying life. When she begins to live with less depressing, she will likely credit her improvement to vitamins or herbal tea rather than to Phyllis's intervention, but what she believes is much less important than the fact that she will have begun to live more effectively.

To deal with Carol, Phyllis first has to learn one of the most important axioms of choice theory:

Never let people control you with the pain and misery they are choosing.

This does not mean you should reject them, fight with them, abandon them, or beg them. And it certainly does not mean you should not be sympathetic and supportive for many months to someone you know who has suffered a personal tragedy. But what it does mean is that, difficult as this is at first, you should deal with long-term sufferers like Carol—who has encountered nothing more exceptional than growing old—as if they were not miserable at all.

For example, when Carol makes her regular morning call to Phyllis and, in her theatrically weak and depressing tone of voice, asks if Phyllis can come over immediately, Phyllis should not respond with her usual immediate promise to make a special trip over as soon as she can get ready. Phyllis should not ask "What's wrong?" because Carol has a list of ready answers that will quickly overwhelm Phyllis's meager defensive question, "Do I really have to come right away?" If Phyllis even hesitates, Carol will say, "I'm too weak to discuss it on the phone." Her voice will then trail off, and as Phyllis yells, "Mom, Mom, what is it?" Carol will just sigh and say nothing, again successfully establishing the urgency of her immediate need for Phyllis.

If, as usual, Phyllis rushes over, she will find nothing different from any previous urgent morning. Carol will go through her usual complaints and fears that no one cares about her and add that she was so faint that she felt that if she hadn't called early, she would not have had the strength to call. She will be a little contrite, saying she knows how busy Phyllis is and that she hates to call. But she will also remind her that if she didn't call, she would not hear from Phyllis from one day to the next—which is not true.

What is true is that Carol has been depressing for over ten years, and Phyllis does not initiate inquiries as often as she did. Carol, however, calls several times a day, always with good reason, so if Phyllis were to call her, it would seem superfluous. When Phyllis does call, Carol has also used the ploy of taking a long time to answer and then telling Phyllis that she had another of her sleepless nights and had just dozed off for a moment when Phyllis's call awakened her. It did not take too many of these experiences to make Phyllis reluctant to call.

Carol is no doubt an expert depresser, but she is far from unusual. Compressing her behavior into a few paragraphs may make her seem extreme, but there are many Carols—young and old, all around us—suffering their lives away in a desperate attempt to take control of someone (or anyone) that they believe they can control with a painful behavior. As long as they can gain some control over someone, they will continue to depress. But even if they cannot gain any control over a specific person (perhaps they live alone or no one pays attention to them no matter how they suffer), they still may continue to depress, because they have not figured out a better behavior. As long as they can gain some control over someone, they will continue to depress. Carol will continue to depress for years even if Phyllis moves away and breaks off all contact with her, because she has depressed for so long that, without some help from someone she cares about, she is unlikely to learn anything new.

Once Phyllis accepts that she cannot let Carol control her with depressing, the first thing she has to do is realize that Carol is choosing all the pain and misery about which she complains. She must never waver from her new choice theory understanding that Carol is not depressed but choosing to depress, or she will be unable to help Carol make some more effective choices. This will not come easily. Carol is an expert at acting as if the most wonderful thing that could happen in her life would be to miraculously get over the depression that has laid her low for years. To begin to deal with her as I suggest here, Phyllis will have to accept on faith that Carol is choosing her misery. But faith will turn to understanding if what I suggest is accurate and Carol does begin to depress less. As she sees Carol begin to make more effective choices, Phyllis will gradually begin to realize that choice theory applies to long-term depressers like Carol as it does to all of us.

When she begins the difficult process of persuading Carol to make better choices, she can expect no cooperation, because Carol will view what Phyllis has begun to do as a challenge to her control, and she will not cooperate unless she believes she is gaining, not losing, control of her life. Right now, Phyllis *is* pretty much her life, so if Carol relinquishes some control over Phyllis, she will have to take control of some other aspects of her life that she has let slide while concentrating all her efforts on controlling Phyllis.

To start, Phyllis must begin to separate herself from Carol's control by setting regular times for her and Carol to get together. No matter what emergency Carol complains of, Phyllis must not run over to her apartment. She should go about this with both subtlety and determination and continue to visit regularly. Once she embarks on the plan, when Carol calls, Phyllis should make a definite appointment to see her when it is convenient to Phyllis's schedule, not Carol's.

For example, in answer to one of Carol's urgent early calls, she should say that she is planning to stop by in the late afternoon and that she will be hungry as her day is too busy to take time out for lunch. She should request that Carol have a snack ready for her when she gets there at about four. When Carol pretends not to hear her, she should repeat herself, saying that after a busy day she is looking forward to the peace and quiet of Carol's place for about forty-five minutes before she has to go home and prepare dinner. No matter what Carol's response to this new procedure (and Phyllis should prepare herself for everything from fireworks to silence), she should repeat clearly when she is coming, how long she is staying, and that she expects a snack from Carol and hang up. If she has to hang up while Carol is talking, she should. If Carol calls back, she should answer once, repeat what she said with kindness, and then either disconnect the phone or not answer it.

When Phyllis gets to Carol's house, she should be warm and caring, but she should stress how tired she is from her busy day, flop down at the table, and ask Carol to get her a cup of tea and a snack. If Carol is in bed, Phyllis should go to the bedroom, say hello, and then, repeating that she is hungry, return to the kitchen and make her own snack. She should do nothing for Carol except call to the bedroom for Carol to come out and join her. If Carol comes out and looks to be waited on, Phyllis should continue to eat her snack and pay no attention except to suggest that if Carol wants something, she should make it and they can eat together. Phyllis should tell Carol that she has been looking forward all day to one of Carol's goodies and that she is disappointed that Carol was in bed. All the while she should take the initiative and chatter about her interesting but exhausting day. As she talks, she should suggest a day and a time for her next visit. As Carol is healthy and ambulatory, Phyllis should try to arrange that next time they do something together away from the house.

She will get many distress calls between this time and the next. Carol will sense that she is losing control of Phyllis and may even make a trip to the local emergency room, complaining of shortness of breath, to punctuate her distress. Phyllis has to go when they call, but even there in the hospital, to begin the long process of teaching Carol that she will not be controlled by dramatic moves like this, she should adhere to their plan to go out together.

In essence, Phyllis's plan is to move from caring for to sharing with Carol. Phyllis should insist that Carol do things for her and for herself and back that insistence up by no longer doing for Carol as she has in the past. Each time she sees her, she should ask Carol to do something small or even fairly substantial that she can still do for Phyllis—for example, make some of her special apple cheese cake for Phyllis to take to a hospital where she volunteers. Phyllis should keep in mind that depressing is not a crippling choice unless it is treated as one. If Carol asks Phyllis to buy her something, Phyllis should counter, if it is at all feasible, by taking Carol to the store and letting her buy it for herself. If Carol has money, she should pay for what she buys. If Carol makes a fuss in a store or a restaurant, Phyllis should tell her that she will not take her out shopping for a month, or some other definite time, unless she stops fussing immediately. If she does not stop, Phyllis should cut the trip short and take her home.

The more Carol does for herself and Phyllis, the less she will depress, because as she regains control over her life, she will need less control over her daughter. Phyllis should encourage her to spend time with friends and get involved in activities. She should back up these suggestions by helping Carol to make the definite plans that are necessary to get beyond talk. These should be extras in the sense that they should not take the place of time Phyllis spends with Carol, but they will become attractive to Carol when she realizes that what she is getting from Phyllis now is all she is going to get. She then has the choice of doing something enjoyable for herself or sitting home depressing. She will depress for a while before she makes a move to do something more effective, but when she finds out that she can depend on Phyllis for so much and no more, she will gradually stop depressing and make some moves. Phyllis has to be patient. This program to move Carol toward more effective behaviors takes time, but my guess is that if Phyllis is consistent in doing what I suggest, she should see progress in less than six months.

Phyllis must be prepared to deal with the variety of new miseries that Carol will create as she becomes aware that she is losing control over Phyllis. Carol will headache, backache, and ache in any and all places that people have learned to ache. She will sick, and if she is a drinker, she will drink more heavily. But if Phyllis keeps in mind the choice theory she has learned, if she puts a picture in her album of herself being a good daughter but not a slave, she will get through the ordeal that Carol is putting her through.

Above all, Phyllis should completely stop asking Carol how she feels. More than any other question, "How do you feel, Mom?" leads right into Carol taking control. When they talk, Phyllis should ask her what she is doing or what she wants to do. She must not get involved in discussing feelings with Carol unless Carol wants to talk about *good* feelings. As I explained in chapter 5, we cannot change how we feel if this component of our total behavior seems sensible—and depressing seems eminently sensible to Carol. To help Carol, Phyllis should focus on what Carol is doing and thinking, because these are components that she can change. Using choice theory, the old as well as the young can be taught new ways, and when they learn them, they are happier for it. I don't want to imply that this is an easy process, but it is easier than what Phyllis has been doing. For years she has chosen to escape into migraining to avoid what to her is the heavier pain of guilting when Carol's demands overwhelm her. As she builds a different relationship with Carol, Phyllis's headaching will cease, and she will have much more energy, since dealing with Carol is draining her.

While Carol is to some extent controlling her own anger at not being able to fulfill some of the pictures in her head, I would judge that most of her pain is directed at controlling Phyllis. There are, however, many people who choose a miserable behavior not so much to control others (although that is always a factor) but to control themselves, especially their angering (which frightens them) at not getting what they want from the world. More than most others, these people will find choice theory hard to accept and very hard to put to work in their lives. I believe, however, that many of them could do it if they made the effort to learn how their misery keeps their angering in check. In chapter 5 I described several people besides Carol who also chose misery. The two people who stand out as those attempting to control themselves are Terri, who washes compulsively, and Randy, the brilliant student who was afraid to go to class.

Terri has an unfulfilling marriage, as many people do. Her husband, John, has no intention of leaving her as Dave left Susan. He is satisfied being married to Terri. It is Terri who is so unsatisfied that she has to wash her hands compulsively fifty times a day with no awareness that this compulsive behavior is keeping her angering at her husband and her thoughts of infidelity in check. She has a picture of love and sex in her head that is not being fulfilled. She also has pictures of staying married for all the usual reasons: children, security, fear of the singles dating scene, and loyalty. But these pictures do not get her the love and sex she desires.

She is in a false conflict—that is, a conflict that could be resolved with hard work—but her choice to wash has made her unaware of this most of the time. She says her marriage is not great but it would be better if she could get over her compulsion. The truth is just the opposite: it is her compulsion that keeps her unaware of how unsatisfying her marriage is. If she is to regain control of her life, she must face the fact that the thing inside her that compels her to wash her hands all day is that she is much more dissatisfied with her marriage than she is willing to admit to herself.

If she were able to learn about the pictures in her head and understand that she is choosing, not compelled, to wash her hands, she might be able to take an honest look at the marriage she has and see how different it is from the marriage she wants. She may never be able to come to grips with the angering that she quickly chooses when she has no effective way to satisfy the sexual urges from both of her brains, but she can learn that she has better choices to deal with her marriage than to wash her hands. Right now, as soon as she gets any awareness of the intense angering that bubbles just below the surface of her life, she washes and keeps it under crazy-clean control.

Like Susan, she must ask herself, "Is choosing to wash my hands getting me what I want from my life?" The answer, as I explained in the last chapter, is always no. In her case, however, unlike Susan's, Terri must also face the unhappy fact that her marriage may be seriously flawed. From the sex and romance standpoint, Susan was not dissatisfied with Dave when he was attentive. She was dissatisfied when he withdrew. Terri's husband does not withdraw. He is very much involved with her, but his involvement doesn't fit her picture of the romantic man she wants. It is possible that he could learn to satisfy her more if she would tell him what she wants, but she has not been willing to do this so far. To her, it is totally unromantic to spell out her desires; a real lover would sense what she wants. It may be that she will never be able to convey her desires to him, but even if she could, he might still be unable to satisfy her. There are many times when, try as we may, we cannot satisfy the pictures, especially sexual pictures, in another person's head.

Theirs is a tragic but not uncommon marriage. There must, however, be better ways to handle her frustration besides hand washing, having an affair (she does flirt, which helps a little, but also frightens her because she has a stay-faithful picture in her quality world), or dissolving the marriage. If she can learn choice theory, she will begin to look for better ways than hand washing to deal with her frustration. For example, to satisfy her need for love, if not for sex, she could begin to do some volunteer work with teenagers. She might find them so open and loving that she can get some vicarious satisfaction from being around them. If she finds a teen shelter or a halfway house or gets involved with a community or church-related teenage group, she may get love beyond her expectations as she shares with and helps the young people.

You might argue that this will not get her the sex and romance she craves, but you should again be aware that half a loaf is much better than nothing. If she shares vicariously or sublimates to get part of what she wants, she may be able to stop washing. She can also read romantic novels (millions of women like her have made Harlequin Books a wealthy company) or watch the daily soap operas on television. These may not work for her by themselves—they are too passive—but if she couples them with active involvement as a volunteer or paid worker with teenagers, she may be able to drop her compulsion completely.

It may be that after a while as a volunteer, she will decide to go back to college to get a professional degree in counseling so she can work at a higher level. If she does, she will put so much energy into this satisfying, nonconflicted activity that for all practical purposes her conflict will be submerged. If her husband is sensible enough to listen to her successes and encourage her to go further, it may even kindle or rekindle a little romance in their relationship.

However, as she stops hand washing and gets involved in all this activity, she may decide that she is now capable of ending her marriage, especially if she finds a man who gives her the romance she cannot get from her husband. As many women like Terri stay as leave. Now at least she has a chance to choose. As long as she was a sick compulsive, she had no chance at all.

With the help of choice theory, Terri could work to gain this understanding on her own, or she could get help. But with or without counseling, she must come to grips with the fact that although her marriage is far from the marriage in her head, choosing misery has been her way to deal with this difference.

Randy, the business-school graduate student in chapter 5, was counseled, but if he'd had access to a book on choice theory, it is possible that he would have been able to help himself. He was afraid to go to class his last year because he did not want to finish. If he finished, he would have to throw himself and his new skills on a world he thought would not give him the high-level job that he pictured in his head. The counseling that worked with Randy was to help him to take charge of his life in school, to deal with the intense panic and overwhelming anxiety that grabbed him when he entered any class. When he came for counseling, he was so out of control that he could not sit in a class for more than five minutes before he literally had to run out to regain a semblance of control.

This is not a book on counseling or psychotherapy, and the rich complexities of a successful counseling relationship cannot be described here. What I will explain is the essence of what went on that led Randy to regain control of his life. As soon as we got acquainted, I asked him if he wanted to graduate and get his MBA degree. We spent some time establishing that, as far as both of us could judge, this was what he really wanted. I was aware that if a student was pursuing a course of study that was not the most desired picture in his head—perhaps because he was obeying a parent or studying for a lucrative but boring career—phobicking could be a way out. He insisted, however, that this was not the case—he very much wanted a career in business. Thus, it seemed sensible for us to plan what he could do to get his degree. He had to take control of the present, and we did not discuss the future extensively except to agree that if he did not graduate, the future would be less than satisfactory.

Together we made an action plan. He would tell his instructors that he was afraid to sit in class because he suffered from a phobia. We felt his teachers would be sympathetic if he told them this and also that he was being counseled for the problem, and they were. He asked their permission to sit in the back of the class near the open door and leave quietly if it became too difficult to stay. He told them he thought that in the empty hall he could pull himself together quickly so that if he left, it would be for only a few minutes. This simple plan, with which he regained some control—he could choose to come and go—of a previously out-of-control situation worked. He almost never left class, and he passed with A grades in both his courses.

But the plan went far beyond passing the courses. What he also discovered was that the pictures in his head demanded that he be perfect and were thus too strict. He was able to change these disabling pictures for less rigorous ones, because it became apparent to him that when he told powerful (to him) people like his instructors about what he regarded as a serious flaw in himself—his phobia—they did not reject him; they valued him as a good student and went along with this reasonable plan. He now could see himself as able to succeed in his field; jobs were not open only to perfect people—they were open to the less perfect like himself. He changed his picture to being less perfect so that when he looked at himself in the real world, he now saw a capable person who could talk to people in power and hold his own.

He got a part-time job during school, stopped phobicking almost completely, and now, many years later, he experiences only short periods of discomfort in unfamiliar situations. He will never totally forget how to phobic. None of us seems able to forget these powerful behaviors. But he knows he has a choice and that a better choice is always available if he will make the effort to figure one out. He is a big success in his career and is very much in charge of his life now. To Randy, a plan to take some control of what seemed to him a totally out-of-control situation and then to change his picture of what he had to be and still retain control was the key.

Mary, whom I described in chapter 5, was also phobic; but unlike Randy and Terri, her phobicking was more to control others than to control herself. In this sense, she was more like Carol in that she chose to be afraid to leave the house as her means of controlling

George, her husband. Her phobicking covered up her fear that if she gave him any freedom at all, he might stray from the marriage. But unlike most people who phobic to control others, she did not so much want his love and support as enjoy exerting her power—the power of agoraphobia is immense. While she was not aware that this was what she was doing, she was aware that she neither loved nor respected him; she regarded him as a weakling because he was so much under her phobicking thumb. George finally got fed up with being at her disposal all day long—even at work—and left her, and because she did not need him except to use him, she had no further reason to phobic. She thought of replacing George with her daughter, but fortunately her daughter was smart enough not to rush in to take George's place. Mary decided in a matter of a few weeks to stop phobicking and start living.

If she had loved George or if she had needed him to take care of her, she would not have stopped phobicking. When George left, she would have stayed home and starved until someone in the family or some social agency stepped in. Phobickers do not usually stop as Mary did, because most of them are much more dependent than she was. What she got from George was someone she could push around, but as the years passed, this was no longer satisfying. When George unexpectedly showed a little spunk and left, she was surprised at how happy she chose to be without him.

While Mary is unusual as a phobicker, she well illustrates the choice theory point that …

When our choice to be miserable does not get us what we want, and we believe that there is a better option to choose, we will quickly give up our misery.

Mary differs from most phobickers in that she believed a better choice was possible—most phobickers don't. As I said in chapter 5, to her friends Mary's cure may have seemed miraculous, but Mary had some insight into why she needed George, and she was lucky he left. No miracles were involved in her cure.

In this country there are many people who behave like Mary, Terri, and Randy. They firmly believe they are suffering from a disease, and almost all of them believe that their only hope to be cured is drugs or a counselor who accepts that they are suffering from a mental illness. As long as they believe that they are sick and are treated and regarded as sick, they maintain control through their disabilities and get worse, not better. The problem is that almost all of the treatment offered to them either supports their sickness or teaches them that they are sick if they do not already believe it. Nowhere is this better illustrated than in the case of Richard, the insurance adjuster who snapped his back at work and has remained incapacitated for the past four years. He has had three back surgeries, hundreds of thousands of dollars in medical care, his back hurts worse than ever, and it is doubtful that he will ever return to work.

When Richard hurt his back, he chose to continue to backache long after it healed, because painful as it was, he gained a degree of control over his life that he had never experienced before. As long as he continued to backache, he was able to engage many physicians representing a wide group of medical specialties from neurosurgeons to physiatrists, as well as a large cast of supporting medical personnel ranging from nurses to physical therapists. This huge and expensive treatment team, which probably numbers over twenty skilled people, is analogous to Phyllis, who was Carol's whole treatment team by herself. The reason I draw this analogy is to point out that although these teams are similar, there is one vital difference. Richard wants to control the medical team that is treating him, but they also cooperate in being controlled by him (really by his backache). This is because a large part of their living is derived from being controlled by countless people like him. Phyllis, on the other hand, hates being controlled by Carol and will jump at a chance to learn choice theory so that she can teach Carol more effective choices and escape from her control.

If the treatment team controlled by Richard had embraced the choice theory of this book, Richard would have had no surgery and no extensive medical care, and his medical expenses would have not amounted to more than a fraction of what he has spent and may still spend, as Richard is far from cured. There are many ways—like administering Amytal to him and seeing him do deep knee bends—to diagnose the fact that he is not physically disabled. He needs to be counseled to take charge of his life without backaching. But Richard's chances of getting the care he needs are remote at this time, because the people he controls with this backache have a vested interest in being controlled. It is analogous to giving an alcoholic alcohol, telling him it is good for him, and then wondering why he does not stop drinking.

Lawyers are another group of powerful and expensive people whom Richard controls with his backache. They too like nothing better than to be controlled by people like him, so he now has access to prestigious law offices where good lawyers treat him as if his backache were the most important thing in the world. He cannot fail to be impressed by the power he has that has moved all these people to get him many thousands of dollars worth of treatment—and because he still hurts, they will get him more if they think they can. Financially, the sky is the limit for medical care, and the more he receives, the greater the lawyers' fees. Even if his doctors are beginning to believe that he is more in need of counseling than surgery, the lawyers will find other doctors who will offer him further surgery, expensive physical therapy, or disability payments.

Richard also has a sense of control over his employer and his wife and family. In short, for four years the whole world has revolved around his backache. In all this time, Richard has hardly seen a bill for all these services—the bills go to his lawyer. And as long as he continues to choose to backache, all this powerful and complicated therapeutic machinery continues to operate.

Even if a counselor is finally called in, she is starting with many strikes against her. She has to teach Richard to choose a better way to live his life, which means giving up the paining. But Richard by now has a vested interest in all that his paining gets for him, and he is unwilling to give it up and return to his humdrum job. In the end he will get over some of his backache when the workman's compensation insurance company finally settles his case. When he realizes that he no longer has any control through backaching, and if he has not been injured by the three surgeries or become addicted to painkilling medication, he will figure out a way to get better. Once someone like Richard is injured in a compensable accident through which legal and treatment teams have a vested interest in being controlled by his pain, machinery is set in motion that seems almost impossible to stop. As I worked for years with many Richards, it seemed to me that once these great medical and legal mills started to grind, it was only the sore back that was important; the fact that it was only one part of a whole man seemed incidental to the process.

In most cases, if you have controlled others or yourself through choosing pain or disability, you can expect little help from anyone who views you as sick. You will get help only from a counselor or family member who understands what you are choosing to do with your life, won't let you control him or her with it, and helps you to find the better choices that are always available. In the beginning you will bitterly resent anyone who does not support your illness and thus escapes from your control. People will give you this book to read, and you will resent both them and the book, because if you accept what is written, you will have to consider giving up the tremendous control you have gained through the painful life you have been choosing for so long.

Whenever you give up control, even painful control, it is neither easy nor quick to replace what you have lost. Like a drug addict without drugs, there is a painful period that you will choose to suffer through as you learn to make better choices with your life. The best thing you can do is stay close to anyone who does not believe you are sick. These are your best friends, and they will see you through the period of transition from pain to responsibility. It is also your choice, if you want to stop miserabling, to take the initiative and tell your friends, relatives, and even professional helpers that you are not sick and do not want to be treated as sick. What you need is their help and support as you learn to work and play without pain or disability. You need laughter, not self-indulgent paining; companionship, not sympathy; and personal accomplishment, not dependence on those who earn a living from your misery.

16. Choosing to Be Healthy

Health care is delivered in this country in a way that causes almost all of us to experience a marked loss of control when we go to a physician for treatment. Except in unusual circumstances, our only responsibility is to present ourselves to the physician as sick. It is then her responsibility to treat us or to direct us to treatment that will make us well or as close to well as possible. There is little or nothing in the present system—either in theory or practice—that encourages or even expects the patient to participate actively in his or her treatment, because almost all control is removed from the patient and relegated to the physician.

But as I explained in chapter 8, most of the long-term diseases we suffer, such as heart disease or rheumatoid arthritis, are psychosomatic in origin; they are caused by our losing control over our lives. Because our present medical delivery system, which concentrates almost solely on physical causes and treatments, has nothing to do with helping us to regain control over our lives, it is generally ineffective for these diseases. It follows, therefore, that the most effective treatment for psychosomatic diseases is what we can do for ourselves to regain control, not what our doctors can do for us. For example, Alan, whom I discussed in chapter 8, suffered a heart attack and remained disabled even after coronary bypass surgery because his life was and continued to be out of control. He would have been much better off if he had depended on his physician less and himself more.

Alan's heart attack did not come without warning. He had been examined regularly by his physician, and while he had no obvious signs of heart disease prior to the attack, he did complain of fatigue and not feeling fit. His blood pressure was on the high side of normal, and the blood chemistries that are thought to be related to heart disease were also in the high-normal range. Still, he got a clean bill of health, accompanied by his doctor's friendly admonition to take it a little easier and keep in close touch if he developed any alarming symptoms.

His physician did not inquire into the way he was presently choosing to live his life or what he might do to take more effective control over a life that a little inquiry would have revealed was seriously out of control. Alan's doctor may have sensed that Alan would not have been receptive to such an inquiry, and he may not have wanted to take the time and make the effort to stray from pure medical treatment to try to teach Alan what is presently well known to prevent a heart attack. So, in a sense, both Alan and his doctor unwittingly conspired to set the stage for his attack. Alan's mistake was to depend totally on his doctor for things that his doctor could not do—prevent his heart attack by treating him medically—and would not do. The doctor did not inquire into Alan's life or prescribe a psychological, exercise, and nutritional program that might slow or stop his progressive heart disease and help him get his whole life back under control.

Had Alan been willing to take the initiative and broach the subject of a total preventive program, it is likely that his physician would have cooperated with him or referred him to a medical program that took these important health measures into account. If Alan had known choice theory, he would have taken this initiative and not settled for the strict medical care that did not prevent his heart attack. If his physician did not want to cooperate in getting actively involved in such a necessary program, Alan would have taken control of his own health by initiating most of this on his own (which anyone can) and making an active effort to find a health-care professional who believed in these sound preventive measures. This is not to say that any one thing he might have done would have guaranteed the prevention of a heart attack, but there is much evidence that when we change the way we live our lives, we can reduce and even prevent heart disease.

To take control of our health, we have to give up the traditional idea that when we get sick, our physicians can cure us. The fact that doctors do cure some (not many) serious noninfectious illnesses is helpful to our health but still does not make the he'll-cure-us approach valid. A major part of our total responsibility is to be responsible for our own health. Physicians should serve as expert consultants to supplement what we can learn by ourselves that will preserve our health. If we get sick, we should not abandon the basic premise that we, not our doctors, are responsible. As much as we are physically or mentally able, we should remain in charge of our own care, with the doctor consulting with us more actively in time of illness. What is more important is that we do not behave one way when well and another when sick but that we continue to be the same. We are always in charge; we may accept more treatment when we are sick than when we are well, but we never turn our lives over to others. When we do, we lose control, and if effective control is essential to health—and I believe it is—we lose the best chance we have to get well and stay well.

We also have to face the fact that although there are exceptions, such as holistic medicine, our present system could be more accurately characterized as a sick-care system than a health-care system. This is because the present payoff for the whole system is in treating sickness;

there is little or no reward, financial or psychological, for maintaining or increasing health. When you visit the huge hospitals that dot our cities, you cannot escape the conclusion that these massive institutions exist because they serve a stream of sick people who are difficult or impossible to cure. If sick people were easily or quickly cured, most of these hospitals would wither away. It is my belief that most sick people are difficult to cure because they are suffering from psychosomatic disease. What is presently offered by the medical establishment removes all treatment responsibility from the patients but in doing so removes the most important element in the treatment of disease: the patients' ability to control their own lives.

Neither Alan nor any of us can wait until the medical establishment begins to accept and teach all of us that responsibility for health, and even for treatment when there is illness, is more the patient's than the doctor's. If this is to take place, it must be initiated by the consumer. There is neither financial nor personal incentive (doctors and hospitals will lose power) for any major part of the medical establishment to do this now. A medical consumer who has put choice theory to work in his or her life will be a person who is prepared to get this process started. Consumers should refuse to accept a medical delivery system that does not recognize that to be healthy, we must take prime responsibility for our own health. When we do, the system will slowly begin to change from sickness care to health maintenance, and our medical bills, which are astronomical under the present sick-care system, will shrink substantially. But, again, this is not the fault of the medical establishment alone; it is our fault for letting others be responsible for our lives.

If Alan had known choice theory, he would have been better prepared to pay attention to the fact that he did not feel well for a long time before his heart attack. The reason he did not pay attention was that he was frightened. Not knowing that there was much he could do to improve his health, he tried to deny the mild but indicative symptoms like chest pain and occasional shortness of breath. He relied on his doctor's vague advice to take it easy and keep in touch, and he tried to reassure himself that his doctor was correct (as he was) in his opinion that at the time of Alan's last examination he was not sick. But Alan was an intelligent man, and he knew that there is a big difference between not being sick and being in good health. Alan was not in good health long before his heart attack, and as his once-healthy coronary arteries slowly eroded and clogged, he still was not sick, by the standards of current medical practice, until the attack. If he'd had a health program to turn to while he still had fairly good coronary-artery circulation, he might have prevented his heart attack.

Actually, there are many good programs, but it is easy to see that they are all based on the premise that we must take charge of our own lives and, in doing so, our own health. In Alan's case, if he had known choice theory, he would likely have done much more to take control of his out-of-control work situation. From his choice theory knowledge of criticism, he would have recognized that if he didn't do something to improve the relationship between himself and JB, his health would be in jeopardy. He knew JB as well as anyone did, and in one of JB's more relaxed and expansive moments Alan could have prepared for this talk by writing down carefully all the very considerable contributions he was making to the success of the business, and when he got together with JB, he could have ticked these off one by one. Then he could have asked JB what else he could do to make the business more successful. No matter what JB said, he should have written it down. Then he should have told JB kindly but firmly that he felt they were not getting along as well as he would like. No matter what JB then said—and it is doubtful that he would have said much to this obviously truthful assertion—Alan should have asked him what they could do to make their relationship better.

At this point JB would probably have had little to say, but if he said anything, Alan should have let him talk and listened. Alan should then have given JB a copy of the list and told him that if he wasn't doing what was on this list as well as JB wished, he would like to talk again privately, and that he had enjoyed the opportunity to get together with him. If JB continued to attack him in front of others as was his practice, the next time he did, Alan would have told him that they must talk privately about the specific problem and then walk away. He would then have told JB that these public attacks upset him and that he did not work efficiently when upset. He might (though it is very unlikely) have gotten fired for this regaining-control approach, but losing a job is better than having a heart attack. Much more likely, however, JB would have respected his polite assertiveness and begun to pick on someone else.

Just as there is nothing in choice theory that says we should choose misery or get sick, there is no reason to remain passive when we are attacked. The best thing to do is defend ourselves sensibly, as I suggest. If we choose to remain psychologically passive, as Alan did, we may lose our health. Once Alan learns choice theory, he will be acutely aware of when his life is out of control, and he will be ready to do something sensible to remedy it. No matter how sensitive to psychological factors Alan's doctor is, he cannot solve Alan's problems for him. Sympathetic listening will help temporarily, and encouraging Alan to face his work problems is even more helpful. But the responsibility is still Alan's. He, not his doctor or JB, is in charge of his life.

The most difficult place to retain control over your life is in a hospital, yet doing so may be vital to your recovery. You should not be passive but take an active interest in all that is being done for you. You should insist that your doctor explain all procedures and that you understand what is going on. If you disagree, you should voice your disagreement. It is not presumptuous to ask the doctor to give you a good reason for what is done if it makes little sense to you. You are not in the hospital to protect tradition or the medical establishment; you are there to find out all you can to help yourself get well. You should be especially sensitive to getting rest and should insist that procedures be coordinated so that you are not continually disturbed. You have a right to expect that the hospital procedures serve you, not them, and it's especially important that you not acquiesce passively while angering inside. Your old brain is working hard enough to get you well; it does not need the added hormonal and chemical burden of anger or fatigue.

You should also do as much as you can for yourself. If there is any way you can help the nurses or aides with your treatment, the more you do, the more effective the treatment will be. The passivity and dependency fostered by most hospital treatment are your enemies, and you must be as active as you can be. Think as much as possible in terms of what you can *do* and as little as possible about how you *feel*. Avoid talking about your feelings to those who visit, because if you see your misery is controlling them, it will be hard to stop choosing more misery even as you are getting physically better. The key again: keep as much control as possible. Your ability to control your life even when seriously ill is your best chance for health. How to stay in charge when you are acutely ill is well described in Norman Cousin's book *The Healing Heart*,[5] in which he recounts his personal battle to remain in control when he suffered a severe heart attack. You can learn much from this valuable book.

When you leave the hospital, work out a detailed recovery plan with your doctor and follow it. Now you have a chance to be in charge, and you should do everything you can to avail yourself of this chance. If you have to stay home, do not stay in bed unless you don't have the strength to get up. Get dressed and engage yourself in some worthwhile activity. When you get tired, go back to bed and rest or nap until you feel refreshed. Push to the limits of your physical restrictions and always ask the doctor if you can do more. Question the value of any long-term medication, and do not take any addicting drug for a protracted period. Try to use as little medication as possible, because all medication has dangers. But if you are convinced that the medicine prescribed for you has a substantial body of research evidence to support its efficacy, take it faithfully for as long as it can be justified to you that you need it.

To be healthy is far different from not being sick. Health means to feel good, strong, alert, rested, mentally sharp, and physically active. Health means to look forward to challenge, both mental and physical. It means time passes quickly rather than dragging. Only you can assess your health. Doctors can only tell you that you have no observable illness, which is a far cry from health. To be healthy, you must have good control of your life; and to help you maintain this control, it is important to have a regular relaxing time each day, which I would like to call an in-control time. It does not matter what you do—a pleasant nap, a long hot shower, a regular after-work get-together, even a hard tennis game can be very relaxing. But whatever it is that you do, for at least thirty minutes each day you should try to do exactly what you want to do.

Remember a time when you were playing Monopoly and had hotels all over the board? Almost every roll of the dice brought in money, and you were safe almost everywhere you landed. Even though you were the obvious winner, you went on playing, magnanimously lending money and taking over distressed property from other players. You chose to be so relaxed, so generous, and so easy to get along with because you were in charge. Your needs for power, fun, and belonging were being wonderfully met by winning this ingenious game, and if you had a cold when you started, you probably didn't even blow your nose as long as you were winning.

To be healthy, we need times like this, and one important lack in Alan's life was that he did not take this important daily in-control time. He tended to be intimidated by JB into working late and then hurried home to a family that was often disgruntled because he was late. He would then anger at them because they didn't understand what he was going through with JB. One of the important things he has to negotiate with JB is better working hours. He needs more time off or he never will get the daily relaxation that we all need to be healthy. Alan, being highly competitive, will probably choose to relax with a competitive game like tennis or racquetball. If so, he must play with people who are about equal to him in skill; otherwise, the pain of losing or the boredom of easy winning will take much of the benefit out of the activity. For any game to be an in-charge activity, however, the game itself, regardless of winning or losing, has to be enjoyable. It is hard for any game to be consistently satisfying if we don't win our fair share.

But beyond winning, what makes any game satisfying enough for it to be an in-charge activity is that we must enjoy the company of the people we play with. While learning, I played tennis for years with a man who beat me consistently, but I was so grateful that such a good player was patient enough to play with me that for a long time losing was satisfying. He was not only a scrupulously fair player who called all the lines accurately but also the kind of person I enjoyed talking with between sets. If our in-charge time is an activity that involves others, they have to be satisfying to be with even if some days the activity does not work out well. There is no guarantee that any game—tennis, golf, or even cards—will always be good. So for the game to be called in-charge time for us there must be a guarantee that the people with whom we play are consistently enjoyable.

Whatever the activity, the time we spend doing it has to be long enough for us to relax completely. It must also be a time when the difference between what we want and what we have is so small that we feel no urge to do anything else. As the new brain relaxes, the whole body will also relax. Even strenuous exercise can be a mentally relaxing activity if it is what we want to do at the time. There is obviously no set minimum of in-charge time that is right for everyone, but my guess is that for good health we all could use a half-hour a day, and more would be better. If it is regular, however, even five minutes of complete relaxation can do wonders for a busy person, such as a mother with small children. For those lucky enough to be able to do it, a three-minute catnap also can provide invaluable relaxation.

For the in-charge time to be effective, what we do must satisfy a single clear picture in our heads and never be a time when we experience any conflict. For example, if I want to play tennis, I play with nothing else in mind. If I want to sit and gaze at the TV, this is what I do and all I do. It does not have to be the same activity each day, but it must occur each day, and if it is with others, whatever the activity, they should all be people we enjoy. If we use alcohol during this time (many people like a drink to help them unwind when the day is over), then the situation where we drink, either home or at a bar, must be so satisfying that even if we choose not to drink, we still feel in charge. Alcohol can enhance the in-charge time, but if alcohol is necessary to get the relaxed feeling of control, this is not the healthy in-charge time I am trying to describe.

Many people have asked me if sex would fulfill these requirements. The answer is that if it is satisfying to both partners, it would be excellent. But since sexual satisfaction depends on so many factors that are hard to control, if I were looking for an in-charge activity, I would not depend completely on sex; it is a wonderful extra to add to our in-charge time. Few of us have too much relaxation, but we should depend on activities that are much more under our control than an intimate relationship is. Reading, especially before bedtime, is an example of an activity that is almost completely under our control. We can do it almost every night, and if it is satisfying, it fulfills the requirements for this time perfectly. On the other hand, while going to the theater or to concerts is very enjoyable, there are so many real frustrations attached to these complex activities, such as great expense and mediocre performances, that they cannot be depended upon to provide the regular in-charge time we need.

Whatever the activity or activities, they should neither depend completely on a certain person nor require a great deal of effort or expense to carry out. This means that if you play tennis or golf, you must be able to afford to play, you must take the time to play, and you must have a few regular people whom you enjoy playing with. In-charge time can also be a hobby that you devote yourself to regularly and that you occasionally share with others; but the hobby, not the others, must provide the satisfaction. This is why there are so many hobbies—they all provide this time easily on a regular basis.

Although I don't do it regularly, I am walking the dog more than I used to, and I find this to be an excellent in-charge time. I write mostly at home, and when I am tired of working, I take the hound for a walk and feel relaxed and renewed after a half-hour stroll down the same street. It is a welcome break from what I am doing, and as a willing companion, the dog is perfect—she has never turned down an invitation to a walk, and I don't expect that she ever will.

With this brief description, you should have no difficulty understanding what an in-charge activity is, but it is easy to persuade yourself that you have this kind of a time when you may not. It is more than a rest, a game, or time away from work; it is a daily time when you feel a deep sense of control because you are doing what you want to do and no one is disputing your right to do it.

It is much harder to find this time without chemicals than most of us realize. Would all of the good times you see on television beer commercials be that good if there were no beer? Does your game—for example, bowling or poker—provide you with relaxation and the feeling of control, or does it frequently frustrate you because the ball does not go where you want it to go or the cards come up wrong too often? Are you willing to make the effort to find the good books and magazines that make reading in bed a high point of the day, a time you look forward to with pleasure?

I believe that not nearly enough of us have this in-control time now. Let's say that both you and your spouse have had a hard and unsatisfying day at work. This does not mean you have bad jobs; it means that few jobs can come close to providing eight hours of satisfying work. As the day progresses, you begin to accumulate a series of frustrations, and at the end of the day these frustrations still rankle. They are not in themselves overwhelming, but like straws on the camel's back, as they add up, they get heavy. To relieve yourselves of these work frustrations, both of you need some time to unwind, and you are both hoping to get this time as soon as you get home. You recognize that there will be more frustrations at home, but before you deal with these, you want to unload the ones you have from work. You are well aware that there is a limit to how great a load of frustration you can carry at one time without losing control and then choosing to anger, depress, or behave in some other potentially destructive way in an attempt to regain it. We all find ourselves snapping at our spouses or kids, not because what they are doing is particularly frustrating but because we add what they are doing to an already heavy load of minor irritations. The whole family has a chance for a better evening together if, for example, one person unwinds with tennis while the other soaks away the cares of the day in a hot tub. Here common sense is good choice theory.

Effective as it is, regular in-charge time has limitations: it will not relieve you of major problems. If your marriage is on the rocks, or your child is very ill, or you missed an important promotion, you will not be able to get this out of your mind because you play tennis or stop after work for a happy hour or two. You must do something active as Alan did when he talked to JB. A good in-charge activity will buy you a little time while you plan, but it is no substitute for satisfying specific pictures in your head. As explained in great detail in chapter 7, it is possible to be extremely frustrated and not sick. There are plenty of painful feeling behaviors like depressing or headaching that we can use to gain some control. But when you are depressing or headaching, you are not healthy as I defined *health* earlier in this chapter.

Creative Take-Charge Time

When I was doing the research for my 1976 book *Positive Addiction*, I became aware that inside of us, if we learn how to tap it, we have a great source of potential strength. Certain simple activities that are actually meditations, such as regular relaxed running, may enable us to tap this potential to the extent that running has helped heavy drinkers to become recovering alcoholics, lifelong migraine headachers to stop migraining, and even those suffering from progressive coronary artery disease to slow the progression. Runners, to cite just one large group of positive addicts I studied, not only gained a great deal of physical strength and health, which was to be expected, but significantly increased their mental strength. I believe they were able to do this through gaining greater access to the constant creativity that is inside us all.

I do not want to imply that to be creative we *need* to become positively addicted; most highly creative people are not. And meditating does not guarantee that we will gain any useful creativity. Driven by the differences between the pictures in our heads and what we have, we all tap our creativity all the time, and many times with powerful results. Sitting relaxed and happy at this computer— which, for me, takes all the drudgery out of writing—I constantly get new ideas. I gear myself up to pay attention to them, and when they come, I often use them. This also happens when I am lecturing to an attentive and supportive group. New ideas constantly and surprisingly pop into my mind, many of them very useful and some of them very funny.

I believe that all of us can gain greater access to our creativity by paying attention to what it constantly provides. Most of the time, however, we are so busy that we either don't pay attention or distrust our creativity. In fact, one of the main differences between great and ordinary people may be that great people pay close attention to their innate creativity and give careful consideration to what it offers. But as we can rarely be too creative, a positive-addiction activity can add a small but important dimension to our lives that is worth considering.

Not all runners or other meditators are sufficiently relaxed and self-accepting to reach the meditative state of mind that gives them access to their creativity. They (runners especially) go after this elusive mental process as if it is an uphill race that they must win, and if they do not reach the standard they are striving for, they criticize themselves and push themselves in a quest for ever-increasing achievement. This may satisfy their need for power and may even become a compulsive behavior to make up for frustrations in their lives, but it does not provide the relaxed self-acceptance that gives them the satisfying sense of achievement that is needed for the activity to become positively addicting.

For example, a good way to tell a meditating runner from a compulsive or competitive runner is that the meditator rarely mentions her activity, because she values its creative privacy, whereas the competitive runner may talk of little else. His shoes, his times, his diet, his body-fat-to-muscle ratios are all his attempts to call attention to the importance of his running. The meditating runner may also race on occasion, but most of her runs are for the sake of running. She prefers to run alone or in the company of another non-competitor like herself. Many runners, however, do both: they run mostly for meditation but also race or run an occasional marathon. Recognizing the difference between the two kinds of running, they keep them separate.

The regular pleasure that can become addicting is the same pleasure you gain when you unexpectedly gain access to your creative process during a time when you are relaxed and in good control. Think of how much fun it is to brainstorm or even just relax and talk to good friends who will listen to your fantasies without putting you down. In all this pleasant activity, the main source of the pleasure is creativity. When we are thinking creatively, we may come up with a worthless or even destructive new behavior, but because there is no need to use it, it comes and goes as a passing thought. Any creative thought that passes through our awareness, however, may be valuable. If we are able to put it into practice, it may help us to gain greater control.

Getting involved in a positively addicting activity is analogous to getting an opportunity to play a slot machine without putting in money: we may win and we cannot lose. Positive addicts gain access to their creativity, which is always pleasurable and potentially strengthening, but are under no pressure to use this access unless it seems to be helpful now or later. Keep in mind, however, that creativity is not necessarily good; all it is necessarily is new. But creativity gained through a positive addiction has a chance to be very good because, being in good control, we will use only creative behaviors that are constructive. Only when our lives are seriously out of control will we, in desperation, accept and put into practice a creative mental or physiological behavior that is crazy or causes disease.

Positive addictions do not come easily or quickly. If you start to run on a regular basis hoping to become positively addicted, you should be aware that for the first six months, at least, you have little chance of reaching this desirable goal. What you will get in just a few weeks, however, is a very healthful in-charge activity. Assuming that you enjoy running and it is relaxing, if you run after work, the small frustrations of the day will quickly drift away. If you run in the morning, you will start out with a clean frustration slate, fresh and ready for work.

But if you make the effort to run regularly three times a week for at least forty-five minutes, after a minimum of six months (but sometimes not for several years), you *may* become positively addicted to this activity. There is no guarantee that you will ever become positively addicted, but if you do, what started as a good in-charge activity will have evolved into an even better creative in-charge activity. Many good in-charge activities—like a hot bath or a social drink after work—will never become positively addicting, because they do not take enough effort or concentration. It is the effort of running and swimming, or the high concentration of a good meditation or yoga exercise, that wipes out all on your mind but what you're doing and thus sets the stage for you to reach a positive addiction. If you succeed in reaching it, it does more than sweep away minor frustrations of the day: it gives you easy access to your creativity. This in turn can provide you with a small but still significant amount of additional strength to help deal with any problems you may have in your life.

To understand this process, keep in mind that creativity is so vital to our survival that our creative systems never turn off. Take a close look at anything you do regularly, and you will notice that you almost never do anything twice in exactly the same way. Our creative systems are continually offering us what may be improvements, and usually without awareness, we try them out. If they work, as they often do, we add them to our behavior with little conscious knowledge that we have done so. But beyond this we are frequently surprised by totally expected flashes of creativity that also confirm that our creative systems are always active.

I believe that it is to gain access to this creativity that people have for centuries engaged in a variety of behaviors that are called meditations. Meditations can be physically active, like running or swimming, or physically inactive but mentally concentrating, like Zen, or a combination of both, like yoga. But active or inactive, they must be single-minded enough that you can do them with no distraction, or they will not work.

Running, for example, is satisfying because runners start with the picture in their heads that they need more exercise. Running becomes a way to get into shape, and they put pictures in their quality worlds of themselves running regularly at least three times a week. It takes time and effort to build endurance, but there is no skill involved; we all know how to run, and any way we do it that is comfortable is good enough. If you are in normal health and run regularly at least three times a week for about forty-five minutes, in three months you should be able to run about five miles in less than an hour. You are not going fast, but even if it takes an hour, it's twice as fast as walking. For running to be a meditation, the first thing to learn is that fast or far is not important; what is necessary is that you run easily. All you need to do is put forth enough effort that four or five slow miles pass before you know it.

If you keep running, your endurance will slowly continue to increase, but how much you eventually gain is not important. What is important is that you see yourself as a good runner gaining in endurance to the point where the miles float easily by and you look forward to your daily run. You will never reach the pleasurable level of positive addiction if you push yourself, because this means that on many days you will be dissatisfied. An addicted runner has good endurance, but she is contented and does not compete with herself or others. As you continue to run and believe more and more that you are achieving what you set out to do, you will find yourself in almost perfect control as you move easily over the ground. Then, on a regular basis, the runner that you see in the real world will be identical to the runner in your quality world.

Because this activity, while it takes effort, requires little or nothing from your mind, it soon becomes an easy, routine, old-brain activity that even the old brain enjoys. If you are satisfied to run for months in this relaxed state of complete control, you begin to experience short periods of time when you seem to lose track of what you are doing. You find that you have covered ground that you do not remember covering. It is not that you were unconscious but that during the easy, routine rhythm of the run your mind slipped away from what you were doing and began to wander by itself. You may also notice a train of thought or a series of thoughts that are totally different from the way you usually think. As you come out of these brief states, things around you may take on a better appearance: trees, flowers, and even sidewalks and alleys may begin to look different and more appealing.

What has happened is that for a brief period you were in the positive-addiction or meditative state of mind. You were tapping directly into your creative system. You were mostly aware of it through new thoughts, but you also noticed that for a minute or two or even a little longer, you felt very good, even ecstatically high. Physically you may get the feeling of power and confidence. It's as if something good has been added to your being that was not there before. For some runners this may not happen while running but immediately afterward, when they are in the state of exhilarated relaxation that usually follows a satisfying workout.

When this happens—and it does not happen often or for long for even the most dedicated runners and those who meditate—you begin to become aware of your own creative system. New thoughts, feelings, and even the suggestion of new behaviors filter into your awareness. Most of these are worthless, but even the brief glimpse into your own undiluted creativity seems to provide a sense of power and confidence that is almost always accompanied by a release of natural opiates that you feel as a burst of pleasure.

Easy running is now so effortless; it is as if you are doing nothing, and it is just this state of effortless achievement, where all that is active is your creative system, that is the meditative state of mind you are trying to achieve. As simple as it is to describe, this is not an easy state to reach. The Zen masters have worked for centuries to find ways to reach this state, which they call *satori,* where for a short time you and the world are at total peace—or, in choice theory terms, where the pictures in your head and the world meld together as if they were one, and creativity is all there is.

You may never realize it, but I am sure that you are using the additional creativity to which you now have access all the time. And as you continue to practice this creative in-charge activity, the altered state of mind lasts longer, sometimes for fifteen or twenty minutes. Runners and others who meditate report that when they are in this state, they get creative flashes that solve problems they were not even aware they were pondering. They admit a lot of creative garbage pops in also, but they separate the creative wheat from the chaff and admit that they even enjoy the chaff. And down the road—who knows? What seems now to be just chaff may turn out to be good wheat grain. As they continue, they find that their minds become fascinating places to visit, and they look forward to these little trips into their own creativity.

Do not feel that you will live any less effectively if you do not have a regular creative in-charge time. Unlike an in-charge time, which I believe we all need, a creative in-charge time, while good, is hardly essential. It is, however, an important choice theory concept that is well worth knowing if you are looking for ways to add strength to your life.

17. How to Start Using Choice Theory

I hope you now understand my explanation of choice theory, but I realize that it is a big step from *reading* what may make sense to you to *using* the ideas in your life. The key to taking this step is not to attempt to make any quick changes in your life. In the beginning, just attempt to look at people around you through a choice theory filter. As you do, the theory will start to become more alive, and what you see people doing, thinking, and feeling will be more understandable. Then begin to look at your own life in the same way, and with little effort you should find yourself beginning to put choice theory to work.

Let me give you a simple-to-understand example of what I mean when I say to look at people around you. I attended many of the nearby university's football and basketball games. The stands are filled with people like us, loyal to the home team, but there is always a small, vociferous group loyal to the opposition. All of us are attempting to satisfy our needs for power, belonging, and fun, and for this we have pictures in our heads of our team winning. When it does win, we choose to feel very good because we are now very much in charge. If our team loses, most of us choose to depress for a short time to control our anger. One mildly inebriated fan, after we won a big game, offered the disconsolate losing fans a jagged broken bottle as they filed out, saying, "Here, you can use this if you want to cut your throat." We all laughed at him, but this simple situation in which control is clearly tied to winning is a good place to observe the variety of feeling behaviors that we all choose when we gain or lose control of our lives. We cheer to encourage our team to greater effort and scream with joy when they do something well. But thousands of us become silent as we lapse into total depressing when our team loses in the final seconds. I cite this game example because everything is so clear-cut and understandable. There is no conflict, and if we win, we satisfy a very definite picture in our heads almost perfectly.

As you observe choice theory in many obvious situations, you will naturally begin to extend this observation to your own life. If you observe yourself failing to get a promotion you wanted, you will see yourself behaving in much the same way you did when your team lost a crucial game. The picture in your head was not satisfied, you were frustrated, and you chose to depress because you lost control. But unlike the game, where the picture of winning fades rapidly, the picture of the promotion persists. If you have settled for just reading the book and have not observed a lot of choice theory as it is used by the people around you, you will find it difficult to stop depressing and easy to blame the boss for your upset. But after you have seen others make a lot of painful choices, you become better able to see yourself choosing what you are now feeling.

You know that if the picture in your head of being promoted is not satisfied and you do not want to change the picture, you have no option but to behave in an attempt to get the promotion you want. You also know that you are choosing your behavior just as you chose to cheer or depress at the game. You are well aware that the course of your life is determined by the pictures you want at the time. You will not give up trying to satisfy these pictures even though, for lack of something better, you may resort to painful or self-destructive behaviors.

As you look at people you know, first try to figure out what the important pictures in their heads are. You may not know exactly what they may be—most situations are not as transparent as a football game—but everyone is always behaving to satisfy his or her pictures, and as you observe someone's behavior, try to guess at what the current pictures might be. Notice how difficult it is for people to change their pictures even though what they want is impossible to obtain. Keep thinking about the pictures you want and see how many pictures you are keeping in your quality world that you have little or no chance to satisfy. Remember that of all the pictures, the only one that cannot be changed or removed is the picture to breathe. Ask yourself, "Am I choosing to be a slave to a picture I can't satisfy?"

Then look at the behavior of the people you are watching. You may have to guess the pictures, but you don't have to guess behaviors. Whether you know choice theory or not, it is obvious that all the happy, crazy behaviors you see at a game are chosen. What you have learned that few people who are not familiar with choice theory know is that when you see misery, that too is a choice. Putting this new knowledge to work in your life will take a long time, because you have had a lifetime of thinking that misery happens to you, and it certainly feels as if it does. But as you look through your choice theory filter at your neighbor choosing to depress to control his wife; your brother, who has never succeeded financially, choosing to drink his life away; or your old aunt depressing for years in a desperate effort to control your cousin, it will gradually become apparent that these are choices. This constant but easy and interesting choice theory observation of the people around you choosing their painful, self-destructive behaviors will help you to accept that you are no different from them. We are all humans choosing pain as well as pleasure as we attempt to satisfy the unrelenting instructions in our genes.

Finally, keep in mind that we have arbitrary control over what we *do*. No matter how much we depress, how painful our heads are, how broken-out our skin, how clogged our coronary arteries, how much we drink, we can always change what we do and think. We can't choose to stop our heads from hurting, to elevate our moods with or without drugs, or to unclog our arteries. We can, however, choose to do something that is more satisfying than these. If we want to make the effort, we can increase our social lives, play satisfying games regularly, study for new careers, and act warm and loving with our families. Valid as the argument may be that we do not feel like trying to change our behavior, we always can. And when we do, if what we do is satisfying, we will always feel better or act in a less destructive manner. The two important concepts to remember are as follows.

First, your pictures in your quality world are yours. You put them in, and you can exchange them, remove them, and add new pictures. You can also choose to concentrate on ones you can satisfy and allot little time and energy to those you can't satisfy but are not yet ready to take out of your head.

Second, whether you directly choose a behavior, such as depressing, or make an indirect creative choice, such as a psychosomatic illness, you always have the option to do or think something more satisfying. You have to breathe, but that is all you absolutely must do. The rest of what you choose is up to you, whether you feel like it or not.

How to Take Charge of Your Life Using your Knowledge of Choice Theory Psychology

Here is a logical process you can follow that could change the course of your life:

- Examine your quality world pictures to see if you have at least one picture that would fulfill each of your five basic needs:
  - survival (safety, security, wellness, and procreation)
  - love and belonging (relationships, connectedness, intimacy, and membership)
  - freedom (independence, mobility, choice, and creativity)

- ○ fun (amusement, joy, laughter, and learning)
- ○ power (control, achievement, competition, and influence)
- Look at your quality world pictures and ask yourself if they are realistic. If not, consider altering them.
- Be sure you know the specific picture in your quality world you are trying to match in the real world.
- Then look at how you are choosing to think and act to get that picture satisfied. Be aware that your feelings and physiology are always a reflection of your thinking and acting.
- Now ask yourself this question: Is what I am choosing to do now helping me create my picture in the real world, or is my behavior hurting my chances of getting what I so desperately need and want?

If your answer to that question is, "I have decided to make better choices in my life, choices that bring me closer to the people I need," then you are ready to begin taking charge of your life. Finally:

- Resolve that you will choose to do one thing today that will help you get what your quality world is urging you to accomplish. It may be as simple as deciding to stop criticizing everyone today, even yourself. The use of relationship destroying external control psychology will impede your progress.
- You can take charge of your life only by choosing to change the pictures in your quality world, or to change what you are doing in the real world. The choice is always yours.

Now you will be well on your way to taking charge of your life if you can put these basic concepts to work, first through a lot of observation and then through personal application. Be patient. You have lived a long time without choice theory, and change is always slow. If you understand that the pathway to practicing choice theory psychology is through the pictures in our heads and the behaviors we choose, you have made a good start. Once these are solidly within your grasp, the rest will follow.

Appendix

Choice theory has been applied in many areas of the helping professions and beyond. The following is a description of such applications.

Counseling and Therapy

Reality therapy was developed as a counseling technique to help people understand themselves and choose more effective behaviors to meet their needs. I developed reality therapy first and later added choice theory psychology to explain why the therapy is effective. My most recent book on the subject of counseling and therapy is called *Counseling with Choice Theory: The New Reality Therapy*. In it I recommend teaching clients choice theory as a way to continue the therapeutic experience by providing them with skills for life. The book *Choice Theory: A New Psychology of Personal Freedom* can also be read and discussed in group therapy facilitated by a skilled counselor.

Relationships

Of the human relationships that are most often unsuccessful, marriage ranks at the top. Currently, half of all marriages end in divorce. The impact on families and all other endeavors that involve people getting along with each other is devastating. Five books address these issues: *What Is This Thing Called Love?*, *Getting Together and Staying Together*, *Eight Lessons for a Happier Marriage*, *For Parents and Teenagers:*

Dissolving the Barriers between Them, and *Staying Together.* These books explain how choice theory can be used to improve every relationship with specific strategies for changing harmful behaviors.

Education

Choice theory ideas have been used to improve the quality of education for students in grades K–12 and beyond for over ten years. There are five books on education, all of which address the pressing issues of student-teacher relationships and competence in the classroom. My most recent book on education is *Every Student Can Succeed.* Also of great value are my other books on education: *Schools Without Failure, The Quality School,* and *The Quality School Teacher.* Based on the Quality School ideas are several resources written by Carleen Glasser for school and educational specialists. They include *My Quality World Workbook* for elementary schools, *My Quality World Activity Set* for middle school, and also *Glasser Class Meeting Kit: Choice Theory Curriculum* for teaching choice theory to all grade levels. *Teaching Choice Theory to High School Students* is a booklet that provides a quick overview of class meetings.

Business and Management

Choice theory has been taught all over the world to businesses and managers. There is a program in Japan that has been successfully training managers for over twenty years using choice theory psychology ideas. The company is called Achievement Incorporated, and it is owned by Satoshi Aoki.

Business people who manage companies trained in his programs report that they are happier, their employees are happier, and their businesses are more successful. The books *Choice Theory: A New Psychology of Personal Freedom* and *The Choice Theory Manager* (published as *The Control Theory Manager*) have been effective tools in teaching lead management techniques.

Criminal Justice and Corrections

For many years choice theory has been implemented in court-mandated diversion programs, by parole officers, and in prisons. Currently a program called the Choice Theory Connection Program has become very successful at the California Institution for Women. Follow-up studies show that, after three years implementation, of the women trained in choice theory, who have been paroled, there has been less than 5 percent recidivism. Choice theory used as a rehabilitation program helps inmates get along better with each other and with the staff and ultimately live happier, more productive lives. The book *Choice Theory: A New Psychology of Personal Freedom* is read and studied at the prison, and recently, the program's Director, Les Johnson, has adopted, Take Charge of Your Life, as a textbook in the curriculum he has created.

Addictions and Recovery

Perhaps one of the most difficult of all human problems to address is the widespread use of addictive substances and maintaining a drug-free life in recovery. Reading the books *Choice Theory: A New Psychology of Personal Freedom, Positive Addiction,* and *Warning: Psychiatry Can Be Hazardous to Your Mental Health*, as well as many of the other books we offer, have been very helpful in the treatment and recovery process. Many who have been helped report that these ideas are compatible with the twelve-step program of Alcoholics Anonymous and do not conflict with any other systems of belief.

Health and Wellness

It is my belief that unhappy people get sick more often. Choice theory offers ideas to help people stay well. In books like *Fibromyalgia: Hope from a Completely New Perspective, Warning: Psychiatry Can Be Hazardous to Your Mental Health, Positive Addiction,* and *Choice Theory: A New Psychology of Personal Freedom*, I address issues of health and wellness through changing the way you think and act, which are components of your total behavior. The other two components of total behavior are feelings and physiology, over which we have no control but which can be indirectly controlled by how we act and think.

Ministry and Faith Traditions

Many religious traditions have embraced choice theory because it is so compatible with their systems of belief. The book *Choice Theory: A New Psychology of Personal Freedom* has been widely read and implemented by people of all faiths.

Research

The William Glasser Foundation for Research in Public Mental Health has been established at Loyola Marymount University in Los Angeles, California, for the purpose of conducting and collecting research on the various applications of choice theory psychology. Currently they are conducting research with their student life resident assistant program, and the psychology department is consulting with and conducting the research being done at the California Institution for Women in Chino/Corona, California. Research is being conducted through major universities all over the world. For more information about the research being conducted using choice theory and reality therapy, refer to the *International Journal for Choice Theory and Reality Therapy* by accessing wglasserbooks.com and clicking the link to the William Glasser Institute.

All books and materials are also available from *wglasserbooks.com*

Notes

1. Glasser, William. *Choice Theory: A New Psychology of Personal Freedom*. New York: Harper Collins Publishing, 1998.
2. Christakis, Nicholas, and James Fowler. 2009, 56–57.
3. Capra, Fritjof. 1996, 243.
4. Gilbert, Dan. 2006, 5.
5. Cousins, Norman. 1979.
6. Smith, Bradley, et al. Assessing the efficacy of a choice theory-based alcohol reduction intervention on college students. *International Journal of Choice Theory and Reality Therapy* 2 [Spring, 2011]: 53.

References

Breggin, Peter. *Reclaiming our children: A healing solution for a nation in crisis.* Cambridge, MA: Perseus Books, 1999.

Capra, Fritjof. *The web of life: A new scientific understanding of living systems.* New York: Anchor Books Doubleday, 1996.

Christakis, Nicholas, and James Fowler. *Connected: The surprising power of our social networks and how they shape our lives.* New York: Little Brown and Company, 2009.

Cousins, Norman. *Anatomy of an illness as perceived by the patient: Reflections on healing and regeneration.* New York: W.W. Norton, 1979.

Cousins, Norman. *The healing heart: Antidotes to panic and helplessness.* New York: W.W. Norton, 1983.

Kohn, Alfie. *Punished by rewards: The trouble with gold stars, incentive plans, A's, praise, and other bribes.* Boston: Houghton Mifflin Company, 1993.

Madanes, Cloe. *The therapist as humanist, social activist, and systematic thinker … and other selected papers.* Phoenix, Arizona: Zeig, Tucker, & Theisen, Inc., 2006.

McGraw, Phillip C. *Real Life, Preparing for the 7 Most Challenging Days of Your Life*. New York: Free Press, 2008.

Pert, Candace. *Molecules of emotion: Why you feel the way you feel*. New York: Scribner, 1997.

Siegel, Ronald. *Intoxication: Life in pursuit of artificial paradise*. New York: E.P. Dutton, 1989.

Simon, Laurence. *Psychology, psychotherapy, psychoanalysis, and the politics of human relationships*. Westport, CT: Praeger Publishers, 2003.

Sperry, Len, Jon Carlson, Judy Lewis, and Matt Engler-Carlson. *Health promotion and health counseling: Effective counseling and psychotherapeutic strategies*. Boston: Pearson Education, Inc., 2005.

Szaz, Thomas. *Pharmacracy: Medicine and politics in America*. Westport, CT: Praeger Publishers, 2001.

Urban, Hal. *Positive words, powerful results: Simple ways to honor, affirm, and celebrate life*. New York: Fireside, Simon and Schuster, Inc., 2004.

Additional References: For more information about the books and articles on choice theory and related topics written by faculty of the William Glasser Institute Worldwide, contact the William Glasser Institute: www.wglasserinst@gmail.com.